HUMANKIND

HUMANKIND

Solidarity with Nonhuman People

Timothy Morton

VERSO

London • New York

First published by Verso 2017
© Timothy Morton 2017

1 3 5 7 9 10 8 6 4 2

Verso
UK: 6 Meard Street, London W1F 0EG
US: 20 Jay Street, Suite 1010, Brooklyn, NY 11201
versobooks.com

Verso is the imprint of New Left Books

ISBN-13: 978-1-78663-132-9
ISBN-13: 978-1-78663-131-2 (UK EBK)
ISBN-13: 978-1-78663-133-6 (US EBK)

British Library Cataloguing in Publication Data
A catalogue record for this book is available from the British Library

Library of Congress Cataloging-in-Publication Data
Names: Morton, Timothy, 1968- author.
Title: Humankind / Timothy Morton.
Description: Brooklyn : Verso Books, 2017. | Includes bibliographical
references and index. |
Identifiers: LCCN 2017011128 (print) | LCCN 2017024047 (ebook) | ISBN
9781786631336 () | ISBN 9781786631329 (hardback : alk. paper)
Subjects: LCSH: Philosophical anthropology. | Human beings. | Animals
(Philosophy) | Human-animal relationships.
Classification: LCC BD450 (ebook) | LCC BD450 .M645 2017 (print) | DDC
128—dc23
LC record available at https://lccn.loc.gov/2017011128

Typeset in Adobe Garamond by Hewer Text UK Ltd, Edinburgh
Printed and bound by CPI Group (UK) Ltd, Croydon, CR0 4YY

For the Water Protectors

Contents

Acknowledgments

I would like to thank my editor Federico Campagna for his brilliant insight and aid. Federico caused such deep and positive changes to my writing that I will be forever in his debt.

My research assistants Kevin MacDonnell and Randi Mihajlovic worked tirelessly helping me to finish the manuscript. Beyond this, Kevin has been my assistant for two years now and my scholarly life is so much better for it. Thank you, Kevin, for everything.

Nicolas Shumway, Dean of Humanities at Rice, deserves a special mention for his untiring belief in what I do. I'm forever in his debt.

So many people shared thoughts and suggestions, kindness and support. Among them were Blaise Agüera y Arcas, Heitham Al-Sayed, Ian Balfour, Andrew Battaglia, Anna Bernagozzi, Daniel Birnbaum, Ian Bogost, Tanya Bonakdar, Marcus Boon, Dominic Boyer, David Brooks, Alex Cecchetti, Stephen Cairns, Eric Cazdyn, Ian Cheng, Kari Conte, Carolyn Deby, Nigel Clark, Juliana Cope, Laura Copelin, Annie Culver, Sarah Ellenzweig, Olafur Eliasson, Anna Engberg, Jane Farver, Dirk Felleman, João Florêncio, Mark Foster Gage, Peter Gershon, Hazel Gibson, Jóga Jóhannsdóttir, Jón Gnarr, Kathelin Gray, Sofie Grettve, Lizzy Grindy, Björk Guðmundsdóttir, Zora Hamsa, Graham Harman, Rosemary Hennessy, Erich Hörl, Emily Houlik-Ritchey, Cymene Howe,

Edouard Isar, Luke Jones, Toby Kamps, Greg Lindquist, Annie Lowe, Ingrid Luquet-Gad, Karsten Lund, Boyan Manchev, Kenric McDowell, Tracy Moore, Rick Muller, Jean-Luc Nancy, Judy Natal, Patricia Noxolo, Hans Ulrich Obrist, Genesis P-Orridge, Solveig Øvstebø, Andrea Pagnes, Albert Pope, Asad Raza, Alexander Regier, Ben Rivers, Judith Roof, David Ruy, Mark Schmanko, Sabrina Scott, Nicolas Shumway, Solveig Sigurðardóttir, Emilija Škarnulytė, Gayatri Spivak, Haim Steinbach, Verena Stenke, Samuel Stoeltje, Susan Sutton, Jeff VanderMeer, Lucas van der Velden, Teodora Vikstrom, Jennifer Walshe, Sarah Whiting, Clint Wilson, Tom Wiscombe, Susanne Witzgall, Cary Wolfe, Annette Wolfsberger, Hyesoo Woo, Martyn Woodward, Els Woudstra and Jonas Žukauskas.

And a big thank you to everyone who showed up to classes and lectures in the last two years. Talking with you is my lab, and there's no way I could know what I know now without you.

Over the years it's become clear that if it wasn't for my many encounters with Jarrod Fowler, I probably wouldn't have written very much; once again I'm beyond grateful to him for his relentless downloading of conceptual quartz crystal powder into something like my head. This book is indebted to the thought of my firned Jeffrey Kripal, whose work on the paranormal and the sacred sparked many thoughts.

While I was writing this book, indigenous people and non-indigenous people in solidarity with them were struggling against the militarized forces of petroculture to prevent the Dakota Access Pipeline in the United States from destroying people of all kinds, whether human or not. They call themselves the Water Protectors. This book is dedicated to them.

There was a time when men imagined the Earth as the center of the universe. The stars, large and small, they believed were created merely for their delectation. It was their vain conception that a supreme being, weary of solitude, had manufactured a giant toy and put them into possession of it . . .

Man issued from the womb of Mother Earth, but he knew it not, nor recognized her, to whom he owed his life. In his egotism he sought an explanation of himself in the infinite, and out of his efforts there arose the dreary doctrine that he was not related to the Earth, that she was but a temporary resting place for his scornful feet and that she held nothing for him but temptation to degrade himself.

—Emma Goldman and Max Baginski, "Mother Earth"

Gosh, you've really got some nice toys here.

—Replicant Roy, *Blade Runner* (Ridley Scott, dir.)

Things in Common: An Introduction

Whoever severs himself from Mother Earth and her flowing sources of life goes into exile.

—Emma Goldman

A specter is haunting the specter of communism: the specter of the nonhuman.

Humankind will argue that the human species is a viable and vital category for thinking communist politics, a politics that this book takes not simply to be international in scope, but *planetary*. By this is meant that communism only works when its economic models are thought as an attunement to the fact of living in a biosphere, a fact that I call "the symbiotic real."

The symbiotic real is a weird "implosive whole" in which entities are related in a non-total, ragged way. (I'll be defining "implosive holism" throughout.) In symbiosis, it's unclear which is the top symbiont, and the relationship between the beings is jagged, incomplete. Am I simply a vehicle for the numerous bacteria that inhabit my microbiome? Or are they hosting me? Who is the host and who is the parasite? The term "host" stems from the Latin *hostis*, a word that can mean both "friend" and "enemy."[1]

Fully one-third of human milk, for instance, is not digestible by the baby; instead it feeds bacteria that coat the intestines with immunity-bestowing film.[2] When a child is born vaginally, it gains all kinds of immunities from bacteria in the mother's microbiome. In the human genome there is a symbiont retrovirus called ERV-3 that codes for immunosuppressive properties of the placental barrier. You are reading this because a virus in your mother's DNA prevented her body from spontaneously aborting you.[3] The loose connectivity of the symbiotic real affects other orders of being, such as language. The opening and closing of suckling mammalian lips around the nipple makes an /m/ sound that is surely the basis of words such as "mamma." Such words are roughly shared by nonhuman mammals, such as cats, whose meows also evoke this action, a sign they learn to use more frequently as adults when they live with humans.

Relying-on is the uneasy fuel of the symbiotic real; this relying-on always has its haunted aspect, so that a symbiont can become toxic or strange-seeming relationships can form, which is how evolution works. The right word to describe this reliance between discrete yet deeply interrelated beings is "solidarity." Without the tattered incompletion of the symbiotic real at every scale, solidarity would have no meaning. Solidarity is possible and widely available because it is *the phenomenology of the symbiotic real* as such. Solidarity is how the symbiotic real manifests, the noise it makes. Solidarity also only works when it is thought at this scale.

In so doing, *Humankind* pushes against the tendency to exclude nonhumans (that is, "the environment" or "ecological issues") from the thought domains mapped out by the academic New Left since the mid 1960s. The reasons for this exclusion have to do with a dominant Hegelian strand within these thought domains, a "strong correlationism" that has now persisted past the moment at which it was tactically useful. The usefulness consisted in how strong correlationism provided ways to draw necessary circles around white Western cultures, clipping the wings of their ideological sense of omnipresence, omniscience and omnipotence. The argument *Humankind* makes has until very recently been left in the hands of conservative forces opposed to "cultural relativism" and "theory."

Conceding an entire region—a very large-scale one at that—to the forces of reaction isn't tactically viable.

Humankind's thinking outside the Hegelian culturalist box requires a number of curious, counterintuitive steps that will deter some readers. This book is very possibly going to freak you out. The byline could be, "Yes, it's possible to include nonhuman beings in Marxist theory—but you're not going to like it!"

WHERE IS THE ECOLOGICAL PRONOUN?

It should be obvious even this early on that one of the principal enemies of what I here call humankind is *humanity itself*. Post-Enlightenment thought is correct to wage war against this counterpart of so-called Nature, a vanilla essence consisting of white maleness. (I capitalize Nature to de-nature it, like frying an egg, revealing its artificial constructedness and explosive wholeness.) Humankind is violently opposed both to Humanity and to Nature, which has always been a reified distortion of the symbiotic real. (I will now begin to capitalize Humanity for the same reasons as I capitalize Nature.) As planetary awareness continues at breakneck speed to interrupt the propagation of the Humanity–Nature dyad, it is tempting to write big-picture books that deceptively address all humans at all times, while predictably arguing for a teleological account of accelerating success and progress toward a transhuman singularity of electronic enhancements to the Humanity substance.[4] Such books are popular worldwide because they *inhibit* the true ecological awareness.

Humankind is an ecological being that can be found in the symbiotic real. Can I give voice to it in this book?

There is no pronoun entirely suitable to describe ecological beings. If I call them "I," then I'm appropriating them to myself or to some pantheistic or Gaia concept that swallows them all without regard to their specificity. If I call them "you," I differentiate them from the kind of being that I am. If I call them "he" or "she," then I'm gendering them according to heteronormative concepts that are untenable on evolutionary terms. If I call them "it," I don't think they are people like me and I'm being blatantly anthropocentric. Ironically, conventional ecological speech talks in terms of "it" and "they," abstract populations stripped of appearances. Ethical and political speech either becomes impossible or begins to sound like deeply fascist biopolitics. Humans even talk about humans that way: "the human race" is an undifferentiated "it." Relying on biology alone would mean defining humans as the best among mammals at throwing and sweating.[5]

And heaven forbid I call them "we," because of the state of polite scholarship. What am I doing speaking as if we all belong together without regard to cultural difference? What am I doing extending this belonging to nonhumans, like a hippie who never heard that doing so is appropriating the Other? As one respondent enjoyed sneering a few years ago, "Who is the 'we' in Morton's prose?"

If grammar lines up against speaking ecological beings at such a basic level, what hope is there?

I cannot speak the ecological subject, but this is exactly what I'm required to do. I can't speak it because language, and in particular grammar, is fossilized human thoughts: thoughts, for example, about humans and nonhumans. I can't say "it" as opposed to "he" or "she," as I've just argued. I can't say *we*. I can't say *they*.

Sure, I can in some sense speak about lifeforms if I ignore the most interesting question, which is, How do I get to coexist with them? To what extent? In what mode or modes? I can practice biology, for example. But if I'm a biologist I base my research on existing assumptions concerning what counts as alive. And implicitly, as a possibility condition for science as such, I'm talking in the key of "it" and "them" rather than the key of "we." So, I haven't made the problem go away.

Right now, in my part of the academy, I'm not allowed to like "We Are All Earthlings," that song by the Muppets, let alone sing it as if it were some kind of biospheric anthem. I'm supposed to condemn it as deeply white and Western, and so appropriative of indigenous cultures and blithely ignorant of racial and gender difference. I'm trying to make the academy a safe space in which to like "We Are All Earthlings." This boils down to thinking hard about the "we."

Ironically, the first scholars in humanist and social science domains to talk about ecology *were* hostile to theory. They latched on to ecological themes so as to leapfrog over what they didn't like about the contemporary academy, which have always been the things I like and like to teach: exploring how texts and other cultural objects are constructed, how race, gender and class deeply affect their construction, and so forth. They wrote as if talking about frogs was a way to avoid talking about gender. But frogs also have gender and sexuality. Frogs also have constructs—they access the world in certain ways, their genome expresses (whether "intentionally" or "with imagination" or not) beyond the boundaries of their bodies. In a strange way, then, the early ecocritics were themselves talking about nonhumans in the key of "it"! In drawing a sharp distinction between the artificial and the natural, they remained well within anthropocentric thought space. Humans are artificers; nonhumans are spontaneous. Humans are people; nonhumans are, for all intents and purposes, machines. The ecocritics have hated me for saying it.

I'm not playing ball with either of these sections of the record store of popular intellectual opinion. I'm not going to leapfrog over theory. I'm not going to keep my trap shut about coral. I'm going to be the devil again, and insist that Marxism can include nonhumans—*must* include nonhumans.

WHAT'S BUGGING MARX?

Economics is how lifeforms organize their enjoyment. That's why *ecology* used to be called *the economy of nature.*[6] When you think of it like that, what the discipline of economics excludes is nonhuman beings—the ways we and they organize enjoyment with reference to one another. If we want to organize communist enjoyment, we are going to have to include nonhuman beings.

Capitalist economic theory is far worse at including nonhumans. Anything considered to be outside of human social space, whether supposed to be alive or not (rivers or pandas), is considered to be a mere "externality." There is no way to include them in a way that doesn't reproduce an inside–outside opposition untenable in an age of ecological awareness, in which categories such as "away" have evaporated. One doesn't throw a candy wrapper away—one drops it on Mount Everest. Capitalist economics is an anthropocentric discourse that cannot factor in the very things that ecological thought and politics require: nonhuman beings and unfamiliar timescales.[7]

Marxism isn't being singled out for special treatment in *Humankind*. Indeed, I'm going to be showing how, with its theories of alienation and use-value, Marxism holds out more promise of ways to include nonhumans than capitalist theory. Such concepts don't so critically depend on a labor theory of value snagged in ideas about property that are ineffective at scales on which humans are just one lifeform among many, beings whose enjoyment considerations are on the same footing.

But in practice, Marxism hasn't included nonhumans. Consider the following sentence, which indicates Marx's commitment to an anti-ecological concept of "away": "The coal burnt under the boiler vanishes without leaving a trace; so too the oil with which the axles of the wheels are greased."[8] And communist solutions to ecological-scale problems have so far strongly resembled capitalist ones: put more fertilizer in the soil, become more efficient . . . This is the kind of thing that reactionary ecocriticism used to observe in the early 1990s: the Soviets and the capitalists are just as bad as the other, green is neither left nor right. So, I understand why it might be disconcerting to find sentences like that one in a Verso book.

Since capitalism relies on the appropriation of what are handily called "externalities" (indigenous lands, women's bodies, nonhuman beings), communism must resolve to not appropriate and externalize such beings. It seems fairly simple put like that.[9] Unfortunately, including nonhumans in Marxist thought will just be disconcerting, and there is a good reason for this.

You can argue about Marx's relation to ecological issues in various ways. The most popular is a theological mode in the key of Hegel: Marx was already there, and he anticipated everything we can now say about ecology. The other approach condescendingly extends Marxism to nonhumans: Marxism is flawed because it doesn't include them, but we can allow at least some of them in, subject to an entry requirement.

Humankind's approach begins by being honest: Marx is an anthropocentric philosopher. But is that intrinsic to his thought? *Humankind* is going to argue that it's a bug, not a feature. What happens when we remove the bug?

The bug was hugely exacerbated in New Left theory domains. Environment is not quite the same as race or gender, because these domains are "strongly correlationist" and therefore irreducibly anthropocentric. Correlationism has been part of the Western philosophical consensus since Kant. It's how science functions, as well as the humanities, so playing with it or rejecting it involves tackling some very deeply ingrained strictures on what counts as thinking and what counts as true. Still, it is being done, the very doing of which might be a symptom of incipient planetary awareness beyond awareness of global capitalism. The speculative realism movement that has been prominent since the mid 2000s might be symptomatic.

Correlationism means that there are things in themselves (as Kant would put it), but that they aren't "realized" until they are correlated by a correlator, in the same way a conductor might "realize" a piece of music by conducting it. The correlatee requires a correlator to make it real: sure, things exist in some inaccessible sense, but things aren't strictly real until they've been accessed by a correlator. For Kant, the correlator is what he calls the transcendental subject. This subject tends to be found hovering invisibly behind the heads of only one entity in the actually existing universe—the human being.

There are things, and there's thing data. Raindrops are wet and splashy and spherical, but this data is not the actual raindrop—it's how you access the raindrop when it falls on your human head.[10] If you think about it carefully, the idea that there is a correlator and a correlatee, and a drastic, transcendental gap between them (you can't point to it), is disturbing. It means, in its most extreme formulation—the one Kant gives but himself ignores—that things are exactly as they appear (they always coincide with their data) but never as they seem (they never coincide with their data). This is a blatant contradiction, and contradictions aren't allowed in conventional Western philosophy.

Kant had accepted Hume's sabotage of the default Western metaphysical concept that cause and effect were easy to identify mechanical operations happening below appearances in some reliable way. According to this, cause and effect are statistical; you can't with a straight face say that one billiard ball *will always* hit another one and "cause" it to move. Kant gives the deep reason for this: cause and effect are on the side of data, appearances rather than part of the thing in itself; they are phenomena that we intuit about a thing based on a priori judgment. If you think this is outrageous or bizarre, remember that this is just exactly the logic of modern science. It's why global warming scientists are constrained to broadcasting a percentage concerning the likelihood that humans caused it. It allows us to study things with great precision, unhampered by metaphysical baggage. But it also means that science can never directly talk about reality, only about data.

Kant unleashed a picture of the world in which things have a deeply ambiguous quality. Now, we could accept that some things can be contradictory and true, and so accept that things are what they are yet never as they appear. Or, we could try to get rid of the contradiction. Kant himself pins down the problem by limiting access to data to thinking—or at least positing thinking as the top access mode—and by limiting thinking to mathematizing reason (regarding extensional time and space) happening within the transcendental (human) subject. Raindrops aren't really weird all by themselves: there is a gap, but it's not in the raindrop (despite how Kant actually puts it when he talks about them); the gap is in the difference between the (human) subject and everything else.

But even this "weak correlationist" gap was too much for Hegel. For Hegel, the difference between what a thing is and how it appears is internal to the subject, which in the largest sense for him is Geist, that magical Slinky that can go up stairs all the way to the top, where the Prussian state hangs out. The thing in itself is totally foreclosed, thought of only as an artifact of the strong correlationist thought space. Abracadabra! There is no problem, because now the subject is the grand decider of what gets to count as real! The gap isn't irreducible; at certain moments in the historical progression of thought it might look as if there is a gap, but not forever. This is strong correlationism. Philosophers have volunteered a variety of beings to be the decider. For Hegel, it's Spirit, the necessarily historical unfolding of its self-knowing. For Heidegger, it's Dasein, which he irrationally restricts to human beings, and even more irrationally (on his own terms, even) to German human beings most of all. For Foucault, it's power-knowledge that makes things real.

Correlationism is like a mixing desk in a music recording studio. It has two faders: the correlator and the correlatee. Strong correlationism turns the correlator fader all the way up and the correlatee fader all the way down. Thus arises from strong correlationism the culturalist idea that culture (or discourse or ideology or . . .) makes things real. The similarity between all the "deciders" is that they are all human—a major error on Heidegger's part, since Dasein is what produces the category "human" as such, not the other way around. You can easily see the circularity in Heidegger's case. Strong correlationism is anthropocentric: any attempt to include nonhumans is ruled out in advance. The correlator has all the power. The correlatee is reduced to a blank screen. Is a blank screen really an improvement on a colorless lump of pure extensionality, which is what things had been according to the default, pre-Kantian, Aristotelian ontology? At least colorless lumps don't have to wait around for whatever movie the decider is projecting onto them to know what they are and how to behave.

Sensitive to cultural difference, the strong correlationist allows other people to include nonhumans, but this also means that these other people aren't very acceptable to them. This dynamic has affected left thinking because strong correlationism got hardwired into it, not only because of the obvious Hegelian strand in Marx, but also because of the strong correlationist lineage of "theory." Foucault studied with Lacan, who was a Heideggerian as well as a Hegelian, for example. Arguments for the inclusion of race and gender along with class were staged from the strong correlationist platform: race and gender are culturally constructed, so rethinking culture—or the restructuring of culture dependent on reformatting the economic structure or base—requires reconfiguring race and gender. Talking about things not coinciding with their correlated appearances might smack of essentialism. Correlatees, seen as "nature," are never seen as part of the mix, because they only exist because of the (human) correlator. These correlatees include humans themselves, thought of as biological entities or as "species," as well as nonhumans. Step one of including nonhumans in political, psychic and philosophical space must therefore consist in a thorough deconstruction of the concept of "nature." It only sounds counterintuitive because of the anthropocentric ways in which we think. The anti-theory philistine ecocritics and the pro-theory "cool kids" are really aspects of the same syndrome. Either nothing is socially constructed, or everything is, and in both cases "socially" means "by humans."

I prefer to throw my hat in the ring with the cool kids. You can't really bomb thinking back to the days before Hume, when, if you were Doctor Johnson, you could kick a stone to refute an argument, as if what those considering how things may not just naïvely exist needed was just a good slap upside the head. The trouble is, turning up the fader on the correlatee—whereas Hegel had turned it all the way down—is ridiculed as essentialism. This might be a way to rationalize a fear that such a move actually *wouldn't* be regressive but simply non-Hegelian, returning thinking not to a state before Hume but to just after him, to Kant. Instead of freaking out and papering over the human–world gap, we could go the other way and allow the gap to exist, which in the end means that Kant's way of containing the explosiveness of his idea must also be let go. In turn, this means that we release the anthropocentric copyright control on the gap and allow everything in the universe to have it, which means dropping the idea that (human) thought is the top access mode and holding that brushing against, licking or irradiating are also access modes as valid (or as invalid) as thinking.

Adorno argues that true progress looks like regression.[11] Stepping outside the charmed circle of the decider is seen as absurd or dangerous, as louche essentialism, as a whole style, not just as a set of ideas. The person who would do that isn't the person you want to be if you're trained in theory class: some kind of hippie. Of course, in reality race, gender and environmentality are deeply intertwined, as the strong correlationist New Leftist will admit when it becomes tactically necessary to talk about the environment as, for instance, a discursively (in the Foucauldian sense) produced feature of social space. But this sidesteps the elephant in the room—the literal elephant in the room. Social space is always already construed as human—the one constructed thing that one can't interfere with is the level at which we start to turn up the fader on the correlatee.

Speaking of hippies, destructuring Western philosophy to include nonhumans in a meaningful way starts to look, from within culturalism, like appropriating non-Western cultures, and in particular the cultures of First Peoples, indigenous people. If it's not possible to cross from one decider's domain to another, it is because they are totally different realities; the correlatee fader has been turned way down to the point where correlatees are only blank screens, so crossing from one decider's domain to another's must violate a basic rule of decorum. Despite the fact that some Western philosophers are allowing non-Western thought to influence them, and despite the fact that this allowance in part disarms the bomb to make the world a safer place, what this looks like to some is doing the unforgivable, gauche, hippie thing of dressing up like a Native American. If I were Oscar Wilde, that deliciously aestheticist and paradoxical socialist, I might archly observe that it looks to the culturalist bad enough to cross over to another's culture without permission, and even worse to be so unstylishly dressed.

These critiques miss the target because they rely on an idea of the incommensurability of cultures. This idea stems from strong correlationism (Hegel). Strong correlationism is equated with imperialism: cultural difference can be used to justify imposing an alien bureaucratic power layer on top of an existing indigenous culture, for example. The critique of crossing over, or of arguing for commensurability, is a symptom of the very imperialism from which one is trying to rescue thinking by departing from strong correlationist orthodoxy. How ironic is that?

One view to which I adhere is object-oriented ontology, or OOO. I have described already its basic move of releasing the anthropocentric copyright control on who or what gets to be a correlator, rather than regressing to pre-Kantian essentialism. OOO has been subjected precisely to this criticism, that it is appropriating indigenous cultures when it talks about nonhumans as "agents" or "lively." It is as if white Western thought is required to remain white, Western and patriarchal in order to provide an easy-to-identify target. The net effect is an ironic situation in which nothing can change, because it would be wrong for someone in that lineage not to sound like that. The Hegelianism structuring both imperialist and anti-imperialist thought domains is like a highly sensitive laser motion detector, stepping over which sets off loud alarms that make it impossible to hear oneself think. As you enter the humanities building, you had better burn the hippie gear you were wearing on the avenue outside and put on the black-on-black costume of stage-hands who see through the naïvety of the actors, or you will end up pathologized and thus incapable of being seen or heard.

But allowing for others to exist in some strong sense, joining their ways of accessing things or at least appreciating them, just is solidarity. Solidarity requires having something in common. But having something in common is exactly what culturalism sees as essentialism, and thus as reactionary primitivism. How do you get there—solidarity—from here—the strong correlationism that lords over Marxist, anti-imperialist *and* imperialist thought domains? Perhaps having something in common is a spurious, dangerous concept? Perhaps we could reimagine solidarity without having anything in common? This is the popular approach from within strong correlationism. Or perhaps—and this is *Humankind*'s approach—we could reimagine what "to have in common" means. I chose the title *Humankind* as a deliberate provocation to those scholars who think that "having in common" is based on ideas that are less acceptable than farting in church.

THE SEVERING

"Solidarity" is an intriguing word. It describes a state of physical and political organization, and it describes a feeling.[12] This itself is significant because "solidarity" cuts against a dominant ontological trend, default since the basic social, psychic and philosophical foreclosure of the human–nonhuman symbiotic real that we call the Neolithic.[13] Let's think up a dramatic Game of Thrones–sounding name for it. Let's call it "the Severing." Why such a dramatic name? What the Severing names is a trauma that some humans persist in reenacting on and among ourselves (and obviously on and among other lifeforms). The Severing is a foundational, traumatic fissure between, to put it in stark Lacanian terms, *reality* (the human-correlated world) and *the real* (ecological symbiosis of human and nonhuman parts of the biosphere). Since nonhumans compose our very bodies, it's likely that the Severing has produced physical as well as psychic effects, scars of the rip between reality and the real. One thinks of the Platonic dichotomy of body and soul: the chariot and the charioteer, the chariot whose horses are always trying to pull away in another direction.[14] The phenomenology of First Peoples points in this direction, but left thought hasn't been looking that way, fearful of primitivism, a concept that inhibits thinking outside agrilogistic parameters.[15]

The starkness of the Lacanian model is itself an artifact of the Severing, derived from Hegel's defensive reaction against the shockwave sent by Kant's correlationist ontology. *Humankind* will cleave closer to Jean-François Lyotard's way of thinking the difference between the correlatee and the correlator. For Lyotard, the real–reality boundary must be spongy. Stuff leaks through such that the real manifests not just as gaps and inconsistencies in reality. There is a loose, thick, wavy line between things and their phenomena, expressed in the dialectical tension between what Lyotard calls "discourse" and what he calls "figure." Figure can bleed into discourse, by which Lyotard means something physical, nonrepresentational, silent in the sense that Freud describes the drives as silent.[16]

Worlds are perforated and permeable, which is why we can share them. Entities don't behave exactly as their accessor wants them to behave, since no access mode will completely shrink-wrap them. So, worlds must be full of holes. Worlds malfunction intrinsically. All worlds are "poor," not just those of sentient nonhuman lifeforms ("animals," as Heidegger calls them). This means that human worlds are not different in value from nonhuman ones, and also that non-sentient nonhuman lifeforms (as far as we know) and non-life (and also by implication the non-sentient and non-living parts of humans) also have worlds.

Something like a permeable boundary between things and their phenomena is highly necessary for thinking solidarity. If solidarity is the noise made by the uneasy, ambiguous relationship between 1 + *n* beings (for instance, the always ambiguous host–parasite relationship), then solidarity is the noise made by the symbiotic real as such. So, solidarity is very cheap because it is default to the biosphere and very widely available. Humans can achieve solidarity among themselves and between themselves and other beings because solidarity is the default affective environment of the top layers of Earth's crust. If non-life can have a world, then at the very least we can allow lifeforms to have solidarity.

But nothing like knowledge of this could leak through a thin, rigid boundary between reality and the real. Such a boundary depends on a smoothly bounded, impermeable human world: on anthropocentrism. How can humans achieve solidarity even among themselves if massive parts of their social, psychic and philosophical space have been cordoned off? Like a gigantic, very heavy object such as a black hole, the Severing distorts all the decisions and affinities that humans make. Difficulties of solidarity between humans are therefore also artifacts of repressing and suppressing possibilities of solidarity with nonhumans.

Children are just as traumatized when a nonhuman is abused in the home as when is a human.[17] A functional definition of "child" is "someone who is still allowed to talk with an inanimate stuffed animal as if it were not only an actual lifeform but also conscious." A functional definition of an adult book is one in which nonhumans don't speak and aren't on an equal footing with humans. The genre of young adult fiction proves the point: the young adult is precisely an anthropocentrist in training. The human–nonhuman separation is expressed as a psychic trauma objectified in the arbitrary definition of "child." The fact that this definition is everywhere in modern global social space indicates the profundity of its violence and the depth of its age. Other artifacts include Freud's concept of psychoanalysis as the draining of the Zuiderzee, turning saltmarsh into farmland (the logical conclusion of which is desertification); or Saint Paul's definition of being grown up, in, "I put away childish things." We are supposed to get behind the idea that playing is a way to adjust to reality, so that eventually we can chuck away the teddy bear like Wittgenstein's ladder. By the age of ten, we have already decided that literature should not be about talking toasters or friendly frogs. Such entities are at best labeled "transitional objects" that allow one to mature from play to reality, itself a telling opposition.[18]

The Severing is a catastrophe: an event that does not take place "at" a certain "point" in linear time, but a wave that ripples out in many dimensions, in whose wake we are caught. We are caught in the Oxygen Catastrophe that began over three billion years ago, the ecological crisis created by bacteria excreting oxygen, which is why you can breathe as you read this sentence. The Oxygen

Catastrophe is happening now. In the same way, the Severing is happening now.

Hiding in very plain sight, everywhere in post-agricultural psychic, social and philosophical space, is evidence of a traumatic Severing of human–nonhuman relations. The difference between modernity and deep premodernity (Paleolithic cultures) is simply that sophisticated technological instruments and contemporary science tell us explicitly that the Severing is produced at the expense of actually existing biospheric beings and their relations. What we are dealing with is a becoming-species, a consciousness that we are humans inhabiting a planet, that has happened precisely as the inner logic of the Severing has unfolded such that, until now, there have been drastic dislocations and distortions in that consciousness and in the concept of "human." We are human insofar as every quality of being human has been severed from a central, neutral substance that Enlightenment patriarchy was happy to call Man.

Intergenerational trauma is a profound topic in psychoanalysis. Children nearing Santa Claus in New York department stores in 2001 (after the World Trade Center attack) were observed to be clutched hard by their parents, transmitting fear rather than love.[19] The grandchildren of Holocaust victims have been observed to suffer from psychological conditions influenced by the traumas of two previous generations. The history of a thing is nothing but the record of all the accidents, whose primordial form is trauma, that occur to a thing. Deep in the structure of the universe are bruise-like concatenations of the universal microwave background that suggest to some scientists an ancient "bubble collision" of two or more universes. Our scientific instruments tell us what old stories told us too, that humans and nonhumans are deeply interconnected. But our ways of playing and our speech say something quite different. The amalgam of these two contradictory planes (what we know and how we talk and behave with regard to nonhumans) must give rise to immense social, psychic and philosophical intensities.

Perhaps melancholia is popular among aesthetes because we carry with us the constantly reenacted 12,500-year trauma of the

Severing. Perhaps this is why Adorno remarks that true progress would look like a regression to the childishly passionate—weeping along with a horse being punished, like Nietzsche, is his example.[20] Humans have indeed been alienated from something, but not from some stable, bland underlying essence—this mythical beast, the lump called Man (and its uncanny spectral shadow, the abject *Müsselmäner* of Primo Levi's Auschwitz, who merely live on rather than surviving in some meaningful sense), is just the by-product of the logic of the Severing. The alienation is a crack in social, psychic and philosophical ties to the biosphere, a hyperobject teeming with trillions of component beings. Our story about how we have been alienated is itself an alienated artifact of the Severing! We have been alienated not from consistency but from inconsistency.

The world of the perpetrator of trauma is drastically depleted. The Severer experiences what one psychoanalyst describes as a desert landscape—a telling image from the overkill intensity of the logistics of post-Neolithic agriculture.[21] It will become highly significant in *Humankind* that logistics are recipes, which is to say that they are *algorithms*. An algorithm is automated human "style," in the very broad sense in which phenomenology means it. Style is one's overall appearance, not just the parts of which you're in control; not a choice (certainly not a fashion choice), but the mode in which one appears, and not just in a visual sense, but in all physical (and other) senses. Style is the past, appearance is the past, a fact that has deep ontological reasons (as we will see). Thus, an algorithm is a snapshot of a past series of modes of humankind, like a musical score. The algorithms that dominate stock trading mean that capitalist exchange is caught in the past: no matter how fast it moves, it's standing still, like the nightmare in which you are running as fast as you can, getting nowhere. The future is foreclosed.

An algorithm is an automated past: past "squared" if you like, because appearance is already the past. "The tradition of dead generations weighs like a nightmare on the brains of the living."[22] To run a society (or anything) purely in an algorithmic mode is to be caught in the past. Self-driving cars will be programmed to save the driver or save the pedestrians if there's an accident: each mode will represent a past state of human style—driving will be caught in the past. PTSD is evidently automated human behavior result-ing from a trauma that ripped a hole in the victim's psyche. The PTSD victim is caught in the past to the power of two. White Western humankind is frozen in the past with regard to nonhumans.

Working with victims of militarized trauma, an analyst argues that the perpetrator has crossed a line of life-binding and life-affirming identifications into a world where the death drive rules.[23] Trauma is experienced as a blank or gap in memory, where the death drive protects the victim against the intensity of the trauma. The Severer inhabits a literal and psychic (and philosophical) desert, from which meaning and connection have evaporated. In the Book of Genesis, the agricultural world is imagined as dust in which the worker labors with great pain, while the preagricultural Eden with its rich affordances is forever sealed off. The inevitability of the sealing-off is itself a symptom of the death-driven agricul-tural program, ensuring, like selective amnesia, that the traumatic Severing cannot be directly experienced, and so not traversed and resolved. It explains why attempts to do so are seen as childish, regressive, or ridiculous—precisely because they *are* appropriate.

A LEFT HOLISM

Solidarity must mean human psychic, social and philosophical being resisting the Severing. This is not as hard as it seems because the basic symbiotic real requires no maintaining by human thought or psychic activity. Western philosophy has been telling itself that humans, in particular human thought, makes things real for so long that an ethics or politics based simply on *allowing* something real to impinge on us sounds absurd or impossible. Solidarity, a thought and a feeling and a physical and political state, seems in its pleasant confusion of feeling-with and being-with, appearing and being, phenomena and thing, active and passive, not simply to gesture to this non-severed real, but indeed to emerge from it. Solidarity is a deeply pleasant, stirring feeling and political state, and it is the cheapest and most readily available because it relies on the basic, default symbiotic real. Since solidarity is so cheap and default, it extends to nonhumans automatically.

Solidarity also restarts temporality. Solidarity means being freed from one's being caught in the past and to have entered a vibrant *nowness* in which the future opens. I will explore this later.

"Solidarity" is a word used for the "fact" (as the Oxford English Dictionary puts it) of "being perfectly united or at one." And solidarity is also used for the constitution of a group as such, the example given being the notorious notion of "the human race," aka species, what is now called the "Anthropos" of the dreaded Anthropocene, a new geological era (officially dated to 1945) marked by human-made materials such as plastics, nucleotides and concretes in the upper layers of Earth's crust.²⁴ Existing thought protocols in the humanities make this geological era look like an embarrassing generalization, an Enlightenment horror that strips historical specificity, race, class and gender from the human. The concept of *species* as such, lurking behind the notion of the Anthropocene, seems violently antique, like a rusty portcullis.

To add insult to injury, solidarity can mean "community," and this term is also compromised by notions of full presence and *volkisch* sentiments. Solidarity presses all the wrong buttons for us educated people. No wonder Hardt and Negri spend so much time finessing it into a diffuse deterritorial feeling at the end of their magnum opus, *Empire*.²⁵ Contemporary solidarity theories want it to be as un-solid and as un-together as possible. They want the community of those who have nothing in common, or a community of unworking or inoperation.²⁶ Heaven forbid that we feel something in common. On the other hand, scholars have become fascinated with the effortless emergence of commonality, as long as it is not too personal; systems, and how they emerge magically from simple differences that, in the Batesonian lingo, make a difference. How the hermeneutical frame of "making a difference" is established in advance (as it must, in order for the differentiating mark to start to work its magic) always eludes systems theories.

We are either resisting an agricultural-age religion by waging war against what we consider to be essentialism; or we are promoting agricultural-age religion by other means, by marveling at the miracle of self-creating entities that emerge from a primordial non-marked chaos. In either case, we are operating with reference to agricultural religion, which is the initial experiential, social and thought mode of the Severing, a massive privatization of access to the real. Only the monarch, a divinely appointed displacement of human powers, has the hotline to a virtual version of him or herself, a further displacement of those powers. Houston, we have a problem.

Why the allergy to positive, juicy, robust-seeming solidarity? Is the allergy itself a symptom of the Severing? Claude Lévi-Strauss describes an experiment in which the upper and lower class of an indigenous society were asked to draw a simple picture of social space. The ruling-class people drew a simple mandala-like form consisting of concentric circles: the inside is differentiated sharply from the outside, and this difference is repeated inside social space. By contrast, the lower-class people drew a circle with a line running down the middle: an internal fissure (black and white, upper- and lower-class, rich and poor . . .).[27]

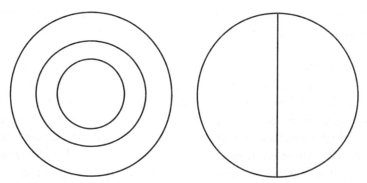

Figure 1. Contradicting Views of Social Space Keyed to Class

The ruling- and lower-class views are radically asymmetrical. Upper- and lower-class people live in totally different kinds of social space: their ontological structure is profoundly different. In the upper-class case, intact, essentialist beings (the "Real People") are surrounded and threatened by forces from the outside that are less human, inhuman, or nonhuman. My use of the term "inhuman" refers to extensionally intimate or proximate parts of what discourse or language or power-knowledge (or Dasein, or Spirit, and so on) classifies as "human" that do not fall easily or even at all under that category. Extensionally spatial proximity is anthropocentrically scaled. Or, what seems proximate to the human morphologically is distinguished finely as inhuman: this is the essence of racism. Via the inhuman a distinction is drawn between the human and the nonhuman that is ontic (you can point to it).[28]

Now we can begin to glimpse the ecological resonance of the ruling-class model, and its traditional agricultural-city format: a walled city, surrounded by fields, surrounded by "the wild." If solidarity can include nonhumans, how can we get there from here without recourse to the ruling-class mandala? Wouldn't solidarity mean being solid, an essentialized ball of elect beings defending against an outside? Where on earth is this outside if social space now includes the nonhuman? Ironically, traditional ecological models rely on the ruling-class mandala structure. These exclude the ecological either by constructing a category of the inhuman, a spectral quality that is neither strictly human nor nonhuman. Nature gets to mean something pristine and pure, an endlessly exploitable resource or majestic backdrop to the doings of the (human) folk.

What is the default characteristic of this thought mode? Let's call it "explosive holism": a belief, never formally proven but retweeted all the time, that the whole is always greater than the sum of its parts. The alternatives are limited. You are a traditional theist or into cybernetics (or any other deployments of this concept); or you are the kind who shows their behind to the political father, as Roland Barthes put it.[29] You are either in church or you are thumbing your nose at church. In either case, there is a church. It's one big reason why talk about populations, which is ecological talk, is considered highly suspicious on the academic left. The population concept definitely has no time for its parts, otherwise known as people such as you and me. This is the utilitarian version of explosive holism, and its near monopoly on talk of species is rightly concerning. But if we can't talk about something like it at all, for fear of sounding like eugenicists or social Darwinists, a left ecology is a fruitless dream. How to proceed?

One very obvious instance of explosive holism is the concept of the invisible hand, developed in Adam Smith's theory of capitalism and first promulgated by Bernard de Mandeville in *The Fable of the Bees*, the subtitle of which is *Private Vices, Public Benefits*. That difference between private and public is a metaphysical difference between parts and wholes that is also a difference between lesser and greater. The invisible hand has evident theistic overtones, conjuring up images of divine providence. Capitalist ideology has relied strongly on explosive holism. The invisible hand concept is emergent and teleological. A benevolent group telos is said to emerge from the selfish actions of individuals. From this teleology springs social Darwinism, which differs from actual Darwinism on this key point, the strong sense of "survival of the fittest," a phrase of Herbert Spencer's inserted into *The Origin of Species* out of fear for the implications otherwise. Selfish, greedy aggression is good in the long run.

The second obvious contemporary instance of explosive holism is fascism. The Latin term *fascis* means a bundle of sticks, expressing the bundling of the folk in a whole that transcends its parts and gives it a firm, constantly present depth. Notice the agricultural provenance of this image: it's not an accident, and not simply in the sense that there is an ideology of the rural versus the urban (black, Jewish, or Islamic social space, and so on). There is an ideology of agricultural social space as such, agriculture as it was conceived in the Fertile Crescent. Agricultural space must be kept together, precisely because of the obvious ways in which, as soon as it starts up, it causes social space to be torn apart: patriarchy, hierarchy, desertification. An underlying aspect of this rip in social space is the Severing, the walling off of human space from the symbiotic real. This walling off gives rise to the duality of humans plus their nonhuman, proprietary cattle (*chattels* and *capital* derive from this term). Cattle are sharply differentiated from humans. This is evidently not how the symbiotic real actually works, via uncanny affiliations that can never be stabilized, bundled into *fasces*.

Does this rip in social space mean that lovely, organic, indigenous (and also explosively) holist Edenic prehistory has been torn apart? Far from it. What humans did was to sever their ties to an *implosive, ultimately meaningless and contingent* symbiotic real. The violence of post-Mesopotamian civilization is precisely not a deracination from Nature. *The violence is the establishment of a human "world,"* cozy, seemingly self-contained and explosively holist, walled off from the disturbing/wonderful paranoid play of the symbiotic real. A world bounded by wild Nature on its physical outside, and by Eden on its historical outside. Humankind is *not* a fragmented being trying to stitch itself back together again into Adam Kadmon or Hobbes's Leviathan. The Severing *consists precisely in the stitching-together itself*, one of whose logical conclusions is fascism; a schizophrenic defense against the void of the symbiotic real. Religion in this sense is the prototype of anti-Semitism, a conspiracy theory (Fall narratives, for example) that provides a reason for the weird palpations and shifty affiliations, the illusory play and physical intensity of the symbiotic real.

Cutting forward an eyelash-flutter more of geological time, what happened is as follows. Neoliberalism turned social space into a wafer-thin sheet through the gauze of which could be glimpsed the wafer-thin sheet of a planet ravaged by neoliberalism. This double void provoked an intense regressive reaction, akin to the schizophrenic defense, in which non-white, non-male humans are dehumanized and made inhuman, thus opening up an Uncanny Valley across whose foreshortened-to-nothing space anthropocentrism sees the decisively nonhuman Other. (We'll explore the Uncanny Valley in greater detail later in this book.)

Inside the mandala of social space, Real People (with essentialist capital letters) exist. Solidarity with nonhumans would be equivalent to allowing nonhumans into a club, of inclusion versus exclusion. If there is no "outside" to actually existing ecological space, since the symbiotic real has no certain center or edge (Where do you, where can you draw the line when you think interdependence?), how on earth does this exclusive club function? If your picture of solidarity is explicitly or secretly based on this ontology of social space, it's not really left-wing, and it's not really going to work—and it definitely won't be able to include nonhumans. The inside–outside difference is foundational to metaphysics.[30] The falsity of an inside–outside model is becoming more obvious as we enter an age of increasing knowledge concerning the seemingly obvious fact that that we live on a planet. Where on earth is "away" when we have planetary awareness? One's garbage doesn't go "away"—it just goes somewhere else; capitalism has tended to create an "away" that is (fortunately) no longer thinkable.[31]

If there is no inside–outside boundary, social space must already include nonhumans, albeit unconsciously. Thus, its contradictions must be structural: they transcend empirical differences. It's not the case that there are "real" or "more real" beings toward the center of a mandala of concentric circles. It's that differences are always arbitrarily produced by acts of violence (social, psychic and philosophical) on beings that cannot in any sense be arbitrarily divided in such ways (hence the violence).

The crack in social space is an artifact of the Severing. Trying to visualize how the world ("reality," or how we access the real) would look if it wasn't there is almost taboo. The taboo means that at some point our visualization defaults to the right-wing circle. Visualize just a circle without a crack—again, this is impossible since there is no inside–outside boundary! Solidarity would then begin to mean something like religious communion, the circle of the elect protected from the beings they excluded in some way. We claim that human solidarity couldn't be like that because we claim that differences are irreducible without violence. But if someone starts considering whether porpoises can be part of revolutionary struggle, some will balk and default to a view that looks like the mandala of concentric circles.

Humankind requires a new theory of violence.

Explosive holism whispers in our ear that religious communion is precisely what solidarity means, because social space is greater than the sum of its parts. And this only works if we cleave in some sense to agricultural religion. And agricultural religion is one of the most basic ways in which agricultural society talks about itself—agricultural society, which is based on the Severing. Our very image of solidarity is predicated on never achieving solidarity with nonhumans!

Solidarity with nonhumans becomes radically impossible: it *mustn't* be achieved, otherwise something very basic will fall apart. You can't get there from here—so "stewardship" and other varieties of command-control (ultimately religion-derived) models of human relationships with nonhumans are also no good for ecological solidarity. Ecological stewardship is ostensibly opposed to anthropocentric tyranny; but both are artifacts of the Severing. Stewardship is the "lite" or less directly coercive (more hegemonic or panoptical) version. One should be the lord over nonhumans, not their tyrant; feudal rather than Assyrian. The capitalist upgrade of this concept is being efficient, minimizing one's impact on Earth; the language that works just as well in the Exxon boardroom as it works in the '70s environmentalist language of "Small Is Beautiful." Small is beautiful because you are part of a transcendental whole—don't rock the boat and make too big a splash in the world. Such thought, often fueled by systems theory, deviates from the feudal and Mesopotamian modes only by acephalically distributing power throughout social space, a biopolitics whose apogee is the Nazi concentration camp. The panopticon is a mandala with nothing in the center, fully automated governance. A social order based on ecology might be the most coercive and oppressive social space ever. The association with fascism is obvious. Do we just give up? Or is something wrong with our theory of solidarity?

Esoteric mandala theory isn't based on concentric circles at all. According to the esoteric theory—the theory preserved in the VIP lounges of agricultural-age religions—mandalas lack a center or an edge; the concentric-circles model is a reification. Esoteric theory proclaims that it's not the essentialism of the right-wing mandala that's the problem, it's the *metaphysics of presence,* which defines essences as explosively holistic. No matter how different and disparate my parts are, as a whole I am Tim all the way through and all the way down. Such a belief is deeply at odds with the symbiotic real.

The struggle for solidarity with nonhumans must therefore include a struggle against the agricultural-age religion that still structures our world, down to the most basic logics of part–whole relations. Western philosophy is a rationalized upgrade of religious discursive space, not unlike how capitalism is an acephalic upgrade of the space of agricultural tyranny. Isn't this maddening quality the Severing in its most stripped-down, zero-degree mode? Pure exclusion, exclusion for its own sake, without empirical beings to point to that are included and excluded? Including nonhumans in this acephalic space of distributed power would be schizogenic. Exclusion would be everywhere, but would apply to no empirical being in particular. It would be right to run screaming from such a vision of environmentalist utopia.

Fully transcending theism and its various upgrades would be equivalent to achieving ecological awareness in social, psychic and philosophical space. It would be tantamount to allowing at least some of the symbiotic real to bleed through. Marx argues that communism begins in atheism, and undermining the Severing by subverting theistic thought modes and institutions would necessarily include nonhuman beings in the march toward communism.[32] Doing so would be tantamount to abolishing at least one gigantic chunk of private property: nonhuman beings as slaves and food for humans. It would be wrong to see this as giving nonhumans rights, because rights discourse is based on notions of private property. If nothing can be property, then nothing can have rights—simply not appropriating nonhumans would be a quick and dirty (and therefore better) way of achieving what "animal rights" discourses machinate over.

We are afflicted not only by social conditions but by the ways we think them, which depend often on a set theory that thinks wholes as greater than the sums of their parts. Such a theory turns wholes— community, biosphere (Nature), the universe, the God in whose angry hands we are sinners—into a being radically different from us, transcendentally bigger, a gigantic invisible being that is inherently hostile to little us. We are about to be subsumed, the drop is going to be absorbed into the ocean; Western prejudices about Buddhism are negative thoughts about explosive holism leaking into the thought space conditioned by that very holism, projected onto Eastern religion. Within this fear of absorption into the whole (along with its ecstatic shadow) we discern the traditional patriarchal horror of the simple fact that we came from others: what Bracha Ettinger calls "being towards birth."[33] Juicing oneself on the uncanny over and over again is a Stockholm syndrome–like repetition (to maintain the rigid real–reality boundary) that we came out of vaginas. The moment at which this fact isn't a big deal, and so no longer uncanny in the sense of horrifying—though uncanny in the softer sense of being irreducibly strange, because it involves undecidable host–parasite symbiotic logics—is the moment at which imperial neoliberal "Western" patriarchal thought space will have collapsed.

Communist theory—theories of solidarity, of organizing enjoyment according to what people can offer and to what people need, without a teleological structure (such as property, class, race, gender or species)— should not be maintaining the thought space of Mesopotamian agricultural logistics. The implications are that serious.

HAUNTING THE SPECTER OF COMMUNISM

It would be difficult to catalog the profusion of communist incorporations of the nonhuman, and the lack thereof. The nonhuman is a vexed place in Marxist theory, somehow with one foot inside and one foot outside—or any number of paws and tendrils, bewilderingly shifting from inside to outside. Marxism is already *haunted* by the nonhuman. Anarchism, that pejorative term for a penumbra of multiple communisms that haunt official Marxism, has done much better than the dominant theory. *Humankind* will be exploring how to add something like the modes of anarchist thought back in to Marxism, like the new medical therapy that consists of injecting fecal matter with helpful bacteria into another's ailing guts. In particular, anarchism helps to debug communist theory of lingering theisms.

There are roughly four incorporation modes. What we need is a synoptic view. The fact that one hasn't been provided yet is evidence that the question of the nonhuman in Marx provokes reactions that are partisan enough to inhibit seeing how the question might be answered: it's difficult to see the wood for the trees. But if the nonhuman were irrelevant, then there wouldn't be any telling burn marks from the partisan heat that forces thinkers into one of four positions without being able to consider the possibility space in which the questions are happening.

Let's divide the thought region into two: Marx either incorporates nonhumans, or he doesn't. We'll call the former "incorporation theory." The most popular form of incorporation theory is what we might call Marx Already Thought of That, or MATT. MATT presupposes that Marx had with great foresight anticipated possible objections to his arguments. These objections consist in assertions that Marx excluded this or that phenomenon from his theory, and MATT says that even if the phenomena don't appear explicitly in Marx, Marx is capable of explaining them. MATT is a charitable houseguest in the Marx residence who feels that even if Karl did miss a couple of plates when it was his turn to do the dishes, the great man will get around to them eventually because his style includes addressing those dishes at some point—so what if he's a bit lazy? He's meaning to wash those dishes. You just aren't giving him the benefit of the doubt, or you have a very limited idea of what dishwashing is.[34]

Actually, this is Strong MATT. Strong MATT is a staunch defender of Marx's dishwashing abilities (and topic inclusion). But Strong MATT has a little brother, Weak MATT. Weak MATT still admires Marx's ability to do the dishes, but he thinks Marx needs a prompt or two on occasion: "Hey, look, you missed a couple of dishes." Weak MATT thinks Marx is perfectly capable of including those dishes in his routine, but Weak MATT doesn't believe that Marx will get around to them in his own good time. Weak MATT doesn't think there's a gap in Marxian theory regarding nonhumans—Marx did already think of them, otherwise Weak MATT wouldn't have a name—but Weak MATT believes that if left to run unchecked, Marx wouldn't get around to talking about them. Weak MATT thinks that adding some nonhumans more explicitly to Marxist theory won't throw it off, because the basic coordinates of the theory implicitly include them.

Thus, incorporation theory has strong and weak versions. The way in which Cuba spontaneously began to grow organic food in 1991, during the Período Especial after the Soviet Union collapsed, might be something Weak MATT is happy about. It wasn't intrinsic to Marxism, but the Communist Party was able to adapt to pressing conditions. Weak MATT recalls that Lenin emphasized the need to flood the soil with as many chemicals as were necessary to sustain agriculture for as many humans as possible.[35]

Now, let's talk about the second half of our ecological thought region, which we'll call "non-incorporation theory." We'll see that non-incorporation theory also divides into strong and weak.

Unfortunately for Marx, the Strong and Weak MATT brothers have a pair of cousins, sisters who are less certain of Marx's ability to pull his weight around the house, the Greek for which is *oikos,* whence we get the word *ecology.* The stronger, older cousin, FANNI, is more familiar to us, because she's popular in the black-and-white thought circles that are definite and rigid about what is the case. FANNI stands for the Feature of Anthropocentrism Is Not Incidental. The older cousin thinks that Marx is an incorrigible anthropocentrist. It's not that he forgot to include nonhumans, or that he already included them but you didn't notice; it's that Marx couldn't possibly include nonhumans at all. Marx didn't forget to wash a couple of plates. He is constitutionally incapable of washing those plates because he only looks around the sink for the dirty dishes and never thinks to examine the dining table. And why should he? The older cousin thinks that Marx's anthropocentrism is a profound *feature* of his thought. What could nonhumans get from Marx? Sweet FANNI Adams, or, if you're American, Fuck All. FANNI can be proud that Marx excludes nonhumans, or upset—it doesn't matter.

Yet FANNI has a younger, weaker and less popular sister, called ABBI: Anthropocentrism Is a Bug That's Incidental. Like her less charitable older sister, ABBI also believes that Marx is incapable of washing those plates and that no amount or reminding will do; and like her sister, she'll never be convinced that Marx was already attending to them, but only we weren't looking. However, ABBI does hold that given the right tweak—say, she injects Marx with a mind-altering drug—Marx will suddenly turn around, notice the plates and start washing them as if nothing ever happened. She believes that anthropocentrism is a bug, not a feature, of Marxist theory. This book was written by ABBI.

What we have done here is make a little logic square. ABBI's position is the inverse of Weak MATT.

BELOW SYMPATHY, BELOW EMPATHY

On July 1, 2015, an American dentist called Walter Palmer shot a lion called Cecil, who lived in Zimbabwe. Facebook erupted. Germany and Gabon tabled a UN resolution against the poaching and illegal trafficking of wildlife. The dentist's address was revealed. He was stalked, shamed, yelled at on-screen and off. Just for a moment put aside thoughts about the common flash-mob moralism that can descend on anyone at any time, like Hitchcock's birds (it's called Twitter for a reason). Consider instead the sheer size and scope of the mob and its emotions. Nothing remotely like that happened during the days of "Save the Whale," the mid to late 1970s. Empathy was what the mob was *performing*—not just a condescending pity or a handwringing helplessness (who knows or cares whether it's genuine). Empathy, as a matter of fact, combined with *action*—again, good or bad, necessary or not, these questions are irrelevant. Sure, Greenpeace started in the 1970s and their Rainbow Warrior intercepted whaling ships. But this was millions of people in the form of a flash-mob Rainbow Warrior going after one very specific person in the name of one very specific lion.

Zambia's minister of tourism, Jean Kapata, complained that the West seemed more concerned about a lion than about an African human: "In Africa, a human being is more important than an animal. I don't know about the Western world."[36] The implication is that the reaction is daft. We'd be right to observe that the reaction bypasses the complex and difficult struggles of African people, or that it's a blip in the society of the spectacle that doesn't address real concerns, or how racism frequently leapfrogs over human beings toward nonhumans—Hitler loved his dog, Blondi, and the Nazis passed animal rights legislation. Identifying with a lion means not identifying with a human.

But does it? There is every reason to ignore the identification, for not only does it appear putatively racist, it's also childish. Cynical reason wants to find aggressive motives hiding within passionate ones, or motives that aren't aggressive enough. We'd be right to observe that this is a good example of human identification with what are mockingly called "charismatic megafauna" and which make up a tiny fraction of lifeforms. But this sort of talk is often made in the key of individual guilt and shame about how we appear to other humans.

Dismissing the incident with Cecil is too easy: there was so much more seething under that mob umbrella than just animal rights or sadistic sympathy. Rights have to do with property and property means "you can dispose of it however you like," which is exactly what the dentist had done, once the lion had been determined (by human fiat, of course) to be something to which he could do what he wanted. Pity is condescending in precisely the way William Blake outlined: "Pity would be no more / If we did not make somebody poor."[37] Sympathy is always a power relationship. This was surely in effect. But so was empathy, which has to do with identification.

One has to wonder whether the "naïve" pre-theoretical upsurge, in all its symptomatic, spectacular-political failure, was an implicit rejection of the idea of, as the Situationists put it, "a holiday in someone else's misery," *whether or not that someone was a human or a lion.* Exactly at its *most* "stupid," the reaction was not about bypassing (African) humans; what it bypassed was the nexus between hunting and tourism, and the way the spectacle the nexus generates keeps an oppressive status quo in place.

Empathy isn't as expensive as we suppose. Since I'm not a spirit in a bottle, facing the problem of how to get out of that bottle to act on things that aren't me, since thinking doesn't exhaust beings anyway, and since thought isn't a privileged access mode, we've been looking for empathy in the wrong place. An anthropocentric place. Maybe it really is easier to identify with a lion than we thought. Wittgensteinian truisms about lion speech (we could never understand one even if one spoke) are, to risk a mixed metaphor, barking up the wrong tree.[38] Understanding, or even being-in-the-same-shoes-as, was never quite the point.[39] The point is that *no effort at all* is required; that whenever effort is brought in, solidarity fades. Adam Smith theorized that aesthetic attunement (reading novels) is a training ground for the ability to identify with other people, and that empathy is the basis for ethics.[40] Identifying with a fictional character raises the specter disavowed by novelistic realism, the specter of telepathy, in which *whose* thoughts and feelings I am tuning in to becomes moot, in which the boundaries between me and another are far less rigid than Western thought has supposed.[41] But why would such an effort of training in telepathy (passion at a distance) be possible at all, if we weren't already an energetic field of connectivity, the symbiotic real and its hum of solidarity? Communist affects are *lower* than empathy, cheaper and less difficult to access, too easy. The point is to rappel "downwards" through the empathetic part of the capitalist superstructure, to find something still more default than empathy.

In a dialectical twist, people are now so immiserated that their kinship with nonhumans starts to glow through the screen of Nature, a construct that since about 10,000 BCE has been the malleable substance of human projects—or its modern upgrade, the screen-like surface onto which humans project their desires. At least some humans are now prepared to drop Nature concepts, to achieve solidarity with the beings that actually constitute the biosphere.

The year 2015 was when a very large number of humans figured out that they had more in common with a lion than with a dentist.

That human–lion solidarity was achieved through misery might incline us not to accept it, though this is exactly how human–human solidarity is achieved. The reason is anthropocentrism. Marx observes how workers are equated with nonhumans, and he describes it as degradation: "As soon as man, instead of working on the object of labour with a tool, becomes merely the motive power of a machine, it is purely accidental that the motive power happens to be clothed in the form of human muscles; wind, water or steam could just as well take man's place.[42]"

One perceived obstacle to accepting nonhumans within Marxism is the way in which Marx describes human production in passages such as this. To encounter the nonhuman within capitalism is to have been stripped of one's human uniqueness. A human being has been reduced to muscles, and muscles have been reduced to replaceable components, simply extensional movement. Consider the examination of Victorian capitalism's micromanagement of the precise minimum space required to live and breathe, from which Marx generalizes:

> [Capital] usurps the time for growth, development, and healthy maintenance of the body. It steals the time required for the consumption of fresh air and sunlight. It haggles over the meal-times, where

possible incorporating them into the production process itself, so that food is added to the worker as to a mere means of production, as coal is supplied to the boiler, and grease and oil to the machinery. It reduces the sound sleep needed for the restoration, renewal and refreshment of the vital forces to the exact amount of torpor essential to the revival of an absolutely exhausted organism . . . What interests it is purely and simply the maximum of labour-power that can be set in motion in a working day. It attains this objective by shortening the life of labour-power, in the same way as a greedy farmer snatches more produce from the soil by robbing it of its fertility.

[It] not only produces a deterioration of human labour-power . . . but also produces the premature exhaustion and death of this labour-power itself.[43]

The macabre final sentence reinforces the sense that what we are witnessing here is a brutal, very real version of scientistic reductionism. Consider how Marx describes a phase of early capitalist primitive accumulation in one witty sentence that also reduces the nonhuman: "First the workers are driven from the land, and then the sheep arrive."[44]

The one nonhuman Marx doesn't put on a lower level is capital as such. What is disturbing about commodity fetishism is that it doesn't require (human) belief; it's fully automated. What is disturbing about the "secret" of capital is not the extent to which it is hidden—even Adam Smith could point out that labor produces value. What disturbs is that its secret *is on the surface*: it is the *secret of social form itself*. In their fascination with content, the bourgeois political economists are blinded. Understanding is irrelevant, and this is the worst that could happen because understanding is the top access mode, since Marx inherited the lineage of Kant. As understanding is associated with the human, nonhuman access modes (brushing against, floating through, licking) are devalued. What is disturbing about commodity fetishism is its autonomous power. So, there is something fundamentally wrong with granting power to nonhumans. Is this idea a bug or a feature?

NEOLIBERALISM AND PLANETARY AWARENESS

The reduction of the human to the nonhuman and the reduction of the nonhuman to the brutal also suggests a way out. An ontology (a logic of *how* things exist) that didn't reduce humans and nonhumans—thus preventing the sour taste that comes from being compared with wind or water—would contravene the implicit logic of capitalism, which makes an ontological noise that exactly resembles materialist reductionism.

Since the UN's Earth Summit (Rio, June 3–14, 1992), what has underpinned the fascist right in the USA has been opposition to solidarity with nonhumans. We can draw many conclusions from this. George Bush the First's announcement of a post-Soviet New World Order is indeed sinister, but so is the fascist interpretation of that announcement. What is fascinating is how explicit the fascists are about it. They combine the Bush administration's image of the New World Order with Agenda 21 of the nonbinding agreement signed by all the one hundred and seventy-eight participants in the Earth Summit to produce a "global banking conspiracy" theory that fuses anti-Semitism and hostility to nonhuman lifeforms.[45]

The first section of Agenda 21 makes noises about reducing poverty and changing patterns of consumption, about containing the explosion of human beings on the planet, and about making agreements in an ecologically "sustainable" way. The second section introduces the concept of biodiversity. The third section delineates the groups of (human) stakeholders involved in Agenda 21's vision. The fourth section talks about implementation. "Sustainability" is the key term, and just as when Goebbels heard the word "culture" he reached for his gun, when I hear the word "sustainability" I reach for my sunscreen. "Sustainability" is an even more vacuous term than "culture," and the two terms overlap. What is being sustained, of course, is the neoliberal, capitalist world-economic structure. And this isn't great news for humans, coral, kiwi birds or lichen. This adds up to an explosively holist political and economic agenda. Individual beings don't matter; what matters is the whole that transcends them.

We require another holism if we are going to think at a planetary scale without just upgrading or retweeting the basic agricultural theological meme, a meme that justifies a human–nonhuman boundary. Fascism is an atavistic reaction to the reality of this oppressive failure, attempting to replace the new god with a fantasy old god, "Making America Great Again." The fusion in the fascist imaginary of Agenda 21 with the New World Order results, as in geometrical triangulation, in a virtual image of an international (Jewish) banking conspiracy. Like the schizophrenic defense of paranoid hallucinations papering over the void of extreme anxiety, the overlap between anti-Semitism and a positive, fleshed-out image of an explosively holist biospheric "international community" defends against the void of actual ecological awareness. The symbiotic real is necessarily ragged and pockmarked.

Yet, a further conclusion to be drawn is something that may sound counterintuitive, and we have certainly heard more seemingly intuitive arguments recently. It seems that racism is underpinned by speciesism. *Humankind* claims that it's exactly the opposite: *racism subtends speciesism.* Finely grained violent distinctions between who gets to count as human and who doesn't generate an "Uncanny Valley" (a term in robotics design) in which the nonhuman (dolphins for instance, or R2-D2) is sharply different from the human: separated from the human by an unbridgeable chasm. If you look out over the chasm at the definite nonhumans, it's as if the chasm doesn't exist. But far from being a thin, rigid boundary that might as well not exist, the Uncanny Valley is a sloppy hole like a mass grave, containing thousands of abjected beings. The Left should take heed that the Far Right underpins speciesism with racism by fusing paranoia about biodiversity with anti-Semitism. The struggle against racism thus becomes a battleground for ecological politics. "Environmental racism" isn't just a tactic of distributing harm via slow violence against the poor. Environmentalism as such can coincide with racism, when it distinguishes rigidly between the human and the nonhuman. Thinking humankind in a non-anthropocentric way requires thinking humankind in an anti-racist way.

We can get there by appropriating and modifying Heidegger's concept of "world." Having a world needn't mean living in a vacuum-sealed bubble, cut off from others. World needn't be a special thing that humans construct, least of all the German humans whom Heidegger seems to think are the best at worlding. We will disarm Heidegger from within. It's not that there is no such thing as world, but that *world* is always and necessarily incomplete. Worlds are always very cheap. And this is because of the special non-explosively holist interconnectedness that is the symbiotic real; and because of what OOO calls "object withdrawal," the way in which no access mode whatsoever can totally swallow an entity. "Withdrawn" doesn't mean empirically shrunken back or moving behind; it means—and this is why I now sometimes say "open" instead of "withdrawn"—*so in your face that you can't see it.*

Everything in existence has a tattered, "lame" world: you can quite easily reach through your shredded curtain to shake a lion's paw, and the lion can do the same. An owl is an owl, and the reason to care for her is not that she's a member of a keystone species; we don't need her to be a brick in a solid wall of world, we need to take care of her, play with her. This gives us a strong reason to care for one another, no matter who we are, and for other lifeforms. It gives us a leftist way of saying that we have things in common. We are humankind.

Now we can see in more detail how strong MATT cheats on Marx and ecology in a correlationist anthropocentric way. Claiming that "Marx Already Thought That" means that ecological politics and ethics amount to "saving the Earth," which means "saving the world," which means "preserving a reasonably human-friendly environment." This isn't solidarity, this is infrastructural maintenance. What is preserved is the cinema in which human desire projection can play on the blank screen of everything else.

The cinema is surely a contemporary version of Plato's cave. The implicit warm, dark, tactile intimacy of such a cave is overlooked if all we want to do is preserve the quality of the shadow play on the walls. And we seem very certain about that shadow play. It has precisely lost a whole dimension of its playful quality, becoming in-flight entertainment, a high-fidelity screen with no flickering, on which we see what we know and know what we see. We don't even have fellow feeling for the puppeteers or the puppets gyrating behind us as we watch, or for the flames that they are tending or the wood the flames require. This is not being trapped in an illusion. It's being trapped in an oppressive and boring *reality* that leaves no space open for illusion and play. The only goal is to maintain existence. It sounds both cruel and tedious.

Attending to the shadows and the flickering flames means that to care for ourselves and other lifeforms beyond mere maintenance of vanilla existence, we will need to embrace a haunting, uncanny, *spectral* dimension. Ecological reality is suffused with a ghostly, quivering energy that cannot be contained as "spirit" or "soul" or "idea" or "concept" without violence. It pertains to phenomena that we call "paranormal," which is easiest to think as action at a distance, non-mechanical causality: telepathy, telekinesis, non-living things moving by themselves—life as a subset of a vaster quivering, movement itself as a subject of a deeper shimmying. To think the human without recourse to reactionary essentialism, to embrace other lifeforms and other humans in solidarity, would need to allow for the possibility of tables that can dance. Such thoughts are taboo in Western metaphysics and culture; and in particular, wouldn't that mean we have to believe something fundamentally wrong? For instance, will we have to accept that the reality of capitalist commodity agency—alienated human productive powers in the form of dancing commodities in the world of exchange value—are here to stay? To submit to a system that doesn't even require belief, only acquiescence? What kind of left ecology is this?

Yes, I really am going to argue that commodity fetishism is saying something true, in a distorted way, about the way things are, the symbiotic real. I really am going to argue, moreover, that consumerism is saying something true about the symbiotic real.

LOSING OUR COOL

Why are we suddenly so interested in humans as a species, and what might need adjusting in how we picture ourselves to ourselves? The main reason is ecological: it's what we have been doing to *other* species that is enabling us to think ourselves *as* a species. Thinking this way supplies the missing piece of the jigsaw of leftist thinking since the 1960s—how to integrate ecology with social revolution.

The New Left unintentionally does what it claims not to. It universalizes the human by distinguishing human beings metaphysically from all nonhumans, in an implicitly pre-Kantian ontological move that seriously weakens, unconsciously, its political edge. Marxist nature means (human) economic and cultural metabolism. Use-value means how a thing appears—for a human. At the very least, other lifeforms should be thought as participating in metabolic economic relations, if not cultural ones. There are octopus economic metabolisms and mountain goat economic metabolisms. The name for all these metabolisms used to be the "economy of nature," which Haeckel compressed into the term "ecology." Ecology names a scale larger than only human metabolisms.

Human economic relations are taken to be the "Decider" that makes things real, that constructs a meaningful reality. Everything else gets to be the same kind of thing, protestations aside: the blank screen for the projection of these relations. Ironically, capitalism for Marx ensures that what these relations produce are relations between commodities that then determine relations between humans. Trees may not have agency, but cans of soup and hedge funds have plenty, another reason for a reflex against the object-oriented view. This is a subtle issue: we are definitely talking about relations between humans rather than relations between whales determining the system that then, when it's capitalism, determines (alienated) relations between humans once again. ("Then" in that sentence is a logical "then," not a chrono-logical "then.") But these relations, whether capitalist or not, are already not humans: they are sets of relations concerning the enjoyment of life, of creativity, of "production." It is simply that the relations are *between* humans. This is worth pondering for one more sentence: what it means is that humans are not exhausted by these relations. Some modes of Marxism might convince you that we're stuck in capitalism forever, forgetting that if there was a transition from feudalism to capitalism, that means that capitalist relations don't exhaust humans. It's just that the nature of these relations make the humans "real"; they "real-ize" them as capitalist or as feudal humans.

Again, ironically, this means that the supposedly anti-essentialist, antihumanist poststructuralist-influenced Left is the last defense of the human imagined as a category decisively separated from the nonhuman. It's perfectly possible and indeed necessary to think nonhumans in a leftist way. Denouncing attempts to do so as "hippie" and denouncing ways of proceeding to do so as "phenom-enological" (the polysyllabic version of "hippie") will no longer suffice.

The trouble is, who gets to decide who or what the Decider is? For a philosopher who was somewhat canny about this kind of truth space, quoting Juvenal's "Who watches the watchmen?", Marx's upside-down Hegelianism contains a glitch that is both logically strange (there's an obvious infinite regress) and politically oppressive. Can we debug the Decider model—can we de-anthropocentrize it?

"Species" means an entity that is real but not constantly present beneath appearances, not constantly the same. "Human" means me plus my nonhuman prostheses and symbionts, such as my bacterial microbiome and my technological gadgets, an entity that cannot be determined in advance within a thin, rigid outline or rigidly demarcated from the symbiotic real. The human is what I call a "hyperobject": a bundle of entities massively distributed in time and space that forms an entity in its own right, one that is impossible for humans to see or touch directly.[46] Here's Marx writing about his concept of species-being in the *Economic and Philosophical Manuscripts*:

> Species-life, both for man and for animals, consists physically in the fact that man, like animals, lives from inorganic nature; and because man is more universal than animals, so too is the area of inorganic nature from which he lives more universal. Just as plants, animals, stones, air, light, etc., theoretically form a part of human consciousness partly as objects of science and partly as objects of art—his spiritual inorganic nature, his spiritual means of life, which he must first prepare before he can enjoy and digest them—so too in practice they form a part of human life and human activity. In a physical sense man lives only from these natural products, whether in the form of nourishment, heating, clothing, shelter, etc. The universality of man manifests itself in practice in that universality which makes the whole of nature his *inorganic* body, (1) as a direct means of life and (2) as the matter, the object and the tool of his life activity. Nature is man's *inorganic body*, that is to say nature in so far as it is not the human body. Man *lives* from nature, i.e. nature is his *body*, and he must maintain a continuing dialogue with it if he is not to die. To say that man's physical and mental life is linked to nature simply means that nature is linked to itself, for man is a part of nature.
>
> Estranged labour not only (1) estranges nature from man and (2) estranges man from himself . . . it also estranges man from his *species*. It turns his *species-life* into a means for his individual life.[47]

Notice the modality of "universal" here: nonhumans can also be universal, just less universal. In this passage, species-being is an interface with the symbiotic real, so intimate that it's an interface between nature and nature. Now, look at what Marx says about species-being a few lines later:

> The practical creation of an *objective world*, the *fashioning* of inorganic nature, is proof that man is a conscious species-being, i.e. a being which treats the species as its own essential being or itself as a

species-being. It is true that animals also produce. They build nests and dwellings, like the bee, the beaver, the ant, etc. But they produce only their own immediate needs or those of their young; they produce one-sidedly, while man produces universally; they produce only when immediate physical need compels them to do so, while man produces even when he is free from physical need and truly produces only in freedom from such need . . .

It is therefore in his fashioning of the objective that man really proves himself to be a *species-being* . . . estranged labour therefore tears away from him his *species-life*, his true species-objectivity, and transforms his advantage over animals into the disadvantage that his inorganic body, nature, is taken from him.[48]

In the second passage, not a page later, only humans get to universalize. We end up with the idea that only humans have species-being. Notice, then, that species-being is ambiguously anthropocentric. It has one foot in anthropocentrism, but one foot not. *Humankind* is arguing that we can lift out the foot standing in anthropocentrism.

The Anthropocene is the time at which the human becomes truly thinkable in a non-teleological, non-metaphysical sense. The waste products in Earth's crust are also the human in this expanded, spectral sense, as if what the human becomes is a flickering ghost surrounded by a penumbra of flickering shadows that seem to hover around it like a distorted halo. This is what we shall call "spectrality." In a weird increase of the amplitude of Derrida's thoughts on the spectral and Marx, we will take spectrality as part of the actual world, not just something that haunts the idea of communism. Derrida leaves the ontological just as it is, which in the end means that big business gets to define the ontological in our age. What happens if we don't leave the ontological alone?

1

Life

I'm—Oh, what is that word? It's so big. And so complicated. And so sad.
—*Doctor Who* (The word is "alive.")

Let's drop the deadly concept of survival. A glance at Primo Levi's *Survival in Auschwitz* shows how the most virulent form of death culture marks a rigid and thin separation between life and death. "Survival" is the key word: This is sheer "living on," yet this is fissured from within between trying not to be dead, and waiting to be dead (the "Müsselmäner"). The fissure is an artifact of the industrial violence done to the victims. When Nazi logistics meets actually existing people, all kinds of uncanny beings "between" the rigid categories of life and death begin to manifest.

Logic doesn't like this very much because logic doesn't like ambiguity. In traditional logic, there is no room for a middle zone, the zone that one encounters in regular "life." Yet actual "life" as opposed to Life with a capital L inhabits this excluded middle zone. What is called "life" is a hesitancy between two different kinds of death: blind machination and total nonexistence. Life as such cannot be opposed to disability. A limb is always a prosthetic limb, an eye is always an artificial one. The engine of evolution is mutation for no reason, such that it is impossible to tell when a new lifeform shows up between a variation and a monstrosity.

But logic, with its "Law" of Noncontradiction and its consequent Law of the Excluded Middle, prohibits the very shades of gray that define small-l life as such. What does this tell us about logic? That it is, as Nietzsche argued, a product of the agricultural age (we live in a version of Mesopotamia) with its patriarchies and its caste systems. Humankind must be thought through this excluded middle, spectral realm between the two kinds of death, not as some idealized living substance. Human life is less spectacular, less grandiose, less vital; more ambiguous, more disturbing and more encompassing. Only then can we think humankind outside of the logistics that resulted in neoliberal capitalism. Let's distinguish this concept of life from other minimal definitions of life, for instance, in utilitarianism or in the notion of sheer sur-vival, or "living on."[1] This is not to oppose mere living on with some whole and healthy bland vitality.

Fragility is a basic ecological category because it's a basic ontological category. If a thing is exactly what it is yet never as it appears, it is broken from within. To exist is to be disabled. Every limb is a prosthetic limb. Creativity can happen precisely *because* of this ontological disability, not in spite of it. Living on is a continual thread, very thin but continual. Creative life is a miracle that can only be achieved by the disabled. Humankind is disabled in an irreducible way.

LIVE EVIL: PATRIARCHAL LIFE AND OBJECT UNDEATH

Life (capital L) is hostile to actually existing lifeforms. This is because of a default ontology, a substance ontology, hardwired into social space. It holds that to exist is to be a constantly present something or other beneath or beyond or despite appearances: over yonder, as in the idea of Nature, which also appeared as a function of an agricultural system.

An algorithm is simply a recipe: take two eggs, beat them, stir in a heated pan with some butter for a few moments—hey presto, a small bowl of scrambled eggs. Settle down in fixed dwellings surrounded by fields, define and repel weeds and pests, maximize the juiciness of your corn kernels at the expense of their flowers . . .

One just needs to leave the algorithm running for a sufficient amount of time, and one can watch as the latest version succeeds in instigating the Sixth Mass Extinction Event. Because humans wanted to avoid the mild global warming of the early Holocene, their algorithm ended up generating far, far worse global warming. Because they wanted to transcend the web of fate and the anxiety-provoking loop structure of being, the Paleolithic realm of the Trickster, humans doubled down, further entangling themselves in the web of fate.

Isn't this the plot of every tragedy? And not surprisingly, because tragedy is a way for humans to compute agricultural logistics; the computation is necessarily limited, as it's a symptom of *agrilogistics*, the logistics of a certain agricultural mode (the Mesopotamian one) and its logical structure.[2] Logistics are how things are organized and implemented; this organization has an implicit logic that is often occluded. The difference perhaps is similar to the one between acting out and being aware. A glance at the way phosphorus, a major agricultural chemical, has affected the biosphere will be enough to convince anyone of the problems of agrilogistics. The tragic mode in which we are caught vis-á-vis the current ecological emergency is an aesthetic product of the very algorithm that engendered the emergency.

How can we find our way out of tragedy space? This is a question that, in a larger context, means, how can we find our way out of agrilogistic configuration space, now requiring industry and computing prostheses to maintain its execution? Life as such is a tragic concept. Just think of poor Oedipus, nailed to the side of that mountain: a little baby, barely alive. Life means *barely alive*.

Agrilogistics has been effective since the beginning: you turn your farmland into a desert, and you move west. Within a short while, patriarchy develops as a direct consequence of agrilogistic functioning. A massively oppressive social hierarchy then emerges rapidly, with its king—Oedipus is a victim of the syndrome associated with incompetent father-kings, which one could name the Laius complex.[3] The history of civilization, which looks like a long retreat from unintended consequences. What is bizarre is how some humans ("Westerners") happily let the program run and run and run, no matter what—it became extremely unpleasant soon after it started. It's even possible that the mild warming of the Holocene was itself caused by large-scale agriculture, thus suggesting that the Anthropocene has had two phases.[4] In either case, what is called Nature is simply the smooth periodicity of Holocene Earth systems. Either this was an artificial construct induced at least in part by humans, or it was a happy coincidence for the construction of the anthropocentric theater of operations, providing a suitably comfortable nonhuman backdrop that agrilogistics could rely on and forget about.

The thin, rigid life–non-life boundary established by the functioning of agrilogistic software is a key component of the world this functioning has created. If we don't like what has happened, we are going to need to find a different concept of whatever a lifeform is. We are going to have to relax the life–non-life boundary. The default utilitarianism encoded into Mesopotamian space contains an implicit axiom: more existing is always better than any quality of existing. This eventually generates the population paradox, discussion of which is significantly taboo even for open-minded, humanistic scholars living within Mesopotamian space. According to this paradox, to have trillions of humans living in a state near to that of Primo Levi's Müsselmäner is always better than to have billions of humans living in a state of absolute ecstasy.[5]

The fact that when you blow it up to this scale it looks totally absurd should warn you that in the time of hyperobjects—the awareness of and the creation of massively distributed beings, of which we can only see little spatiotemporal pieces at a time—this default utilitarianism obviously no longer functions. It wasn't functioning very well in the first place. But now the software has been running for so long, we are able to look at it down a microscope or blow it up to Earth magnitude so as to study it—and, unfortunately, suffer from it.

Control over birth and the birthing body and subjection of women is tied to the default substance ontology and its existence-no-matter-what utilitarianism. Patriarchy intertwines with speciesism and anthropocentrism. Nonhumans, the totality of which are called Mother Earth, are regarded as infinitesimally and infinitely malleable substances; and, in the post-Kantian upgrade of this concept, these substances aren't even substances until humans have formatted them.

More existing at any cost implies a substance ontology whereby objects are mere lumps of extension decorated with accidents. Long before this was formalized (by Aristotle or by reductionist atomism), and thousands of years before the formalization of utilitarianism at the start of the Anthropocene, the default substance ontology was directly coded into social space. Undoing it implies dismantling that social space. The ontological project of dismantling the metaphysics of presence and the anthropocentric definition of nonhumans as manipulable extension units is a political project when considered at this temporal scale—the scale of global warming and extinction.

Mary Daly was quite correct. We live in a death culture, a culture of overkill—Freud's death drive is always a mechanism of overkill—whereby the soft boundaries of plant and animal cells become the rigid, smooth boundaries of plastic, having been turned into oil.[6] We harden and harden the social cell walls quite literally: we use fossilized plant and animal cells to make oil to make plastics such as Mylar and latex, that shiny, smooth, beautiful, protective BDSM membrane. The death drive is precisely the soothing survival mode of agrilogistics, and it is in charge of the concept of Life. The relentless pursuit of relentless life just is death and extermination. The capitalist concept of growth, for example, is a mode of this pursuit.[7]

Art and human sexuality are two of the very few places left on Earth in which the death logic can be played with, subverted, parodied, bent. Sexual selection is even more Kantian than Kant—there is utterly no utilitarian reason for sexual reproduction. Sexual selection is absurdly expensive from DNA's point of view, and sexual selection is done fundamentally for no reason. Arguments that beautiful iridescent wing cases are evidence of a lifeform's virility are circular and question-begging. If being alive was really about just getting on with it and damn the torpedoes of appearance, all lifeforms would be cloning ourselves. There are much more efficient ways of displaying power than having beautiful wing cases. Lifeforms themselves defy the logic that rips appearance away from being.

Mesopotamian social space confronts us with a stark choice between two kinds of death—relentless life (as in the seemingly interminable abortion "debate" over the control of women's bodies) and absolute nonexistence. One can have bland lumps of extension to which you can do anything, sadistically—or nothing at all.

"Life" actually exists between these two deaths. It is a quivering or a shimmering without mechanical input, whereby objects move all by themselves without requiring an external motive force. The quivering is now observable in tiny objects that are nevertheless far larger than the subatomic particles to whose scale such unruly behavior was restricted by the correlationist Standard Model.[8] Another way of saying this is that the intrinsic motility of things implies that appearing and being are inextricable, yet weirdly different at the same time, in defiance of agrilogistic functioning, which also generates the logical "Law" of Noncontradiction that has never been proven formally, because it seems so obvious within agrilogistic social space. Ibn Sina (or Avicenna, the Persian philosopher who flourished around 1000 CE) gets to the point and backs up the law with the threat of torture: that's the spirit, like how Doctor Johnson made a kicking sound and took it to be an argument about the existence of kickable things, or how (slightly more violently) the Inquisition demanded that one confess one's nonbelief in a certain concept and must therefore be burned.[9]

Movement happens because appearance and being slide over one another, are different yet the same, as if being were the loop and appearance were the twist in that loop that creates a Möbius strip. You simply can't tell where that twist begins. There is no nice little dotted line or city wall or hedgerow or concept of inside and outside that will tell you. A Möbius strip is a *non-orientable surface*, by which topology means that it has no inside or outside, no front or back, no top or bottom. A lifeform is exactly this non-orientable entity; if tiny mirrors in a vacuum at absolute zero can emit infrared light without being mechanically pushed, you can have a beautiful wing case for no particular reason, and you can find it sexy just because. The nonconceptuality of Kantian beauty extends at least to beetles and butterflies and fish.[10]

We really, *really* don't like entities to shimmer without mechanical input. Even standard-issue quantum theory wants to limit this disco to the things that exist at or below about 10^{-17} centimeters in diameter. In the sado-thanatological space of agrilogistics, the intrinsic shimmering of being, being shimmering with appearance, is known as a spectral, undead, unholy, heretical taboo or as an esoteric secret given only to those who have made it up to the VIP lounge of agricultural-age religions such as Hinduism or Christianity. Defanged by making it up to the top floor, you are given a heavily mediated version in which you are told you yourself are god, directly, and the point is just to notice that. It's funny, like an iridescent wing case. Axial Age religion can't help sprouting exotic esoteric flowers at the top of its supposedly sensible stem.

In non-agrilogistic space, otherwise known as "Paleolithic" (a pejorative and reifying term) or "indigenous," the shimmering is known as magic. It applies to all objects, whether alive by Mesopotamian standards or not. A First Peoples entity is dead *or* alive, and it's impossible to tell exactly which.

We Mesopotamians are forbidden from stepping outside Mesopotamian thought space. To do so designates you as insane or stupid—for instance, you might be accused of being a primitivist or of appropriating non-Western cultures. All that stuff about how nonhumans have spirits shimmering around them, or is it within them, or is it beside them, is reserved for the distant past and for those who in French are called "*aliens*" (the mad), a telling term for beings beyond the pale, the boundary marker of the agrilogistic dwelling structure. Scoffing or wondering at the idea of foraging for nuts and berries is a displaced way of trying to suppress the ontological shimmering. Whether a shimmering entity is alive or not is impossible to determine without prefabricated concepts. The life–non-life distinction is impossible to maintain; all beings are better thought as undead, not as animate or as inanimate.

In the chapter that follows we shall consider what a species might be without the default substance ontology of agrilogistics. A shimmering, undead, spectral being—an electron, a mouse, a skyscraper, a social movement—is an X-being, intrinsically endowed with superpowers. We can comprehend this precisely through the X that Kant himself uses to describe the one thing he allows to be withdrawn: transcendental synthetic judgments a priori. He calls them the "Unknown = X."[11] But now, release the anthropocentric copyright control on this superpower, and let it belong not just to mathematization of extensional space and time, not only to logical propositions and all other ideal phenomena such as thinking, hoping, wishing, hating (Husserl)—and not only to humans, in the way they ex-sist according to Heidegger and Lacan, but to any entity whatsoever, an idea, a flower, a word, a poem, a tree frog, the biosphere.

There is a term for this flickering, shadowy X-power: the term is *evil.* And as art deals in shadows and specters in excess of what seems implicit in and what emerges from agrilogistic software, agricultural philosophy has very frequently thought it as a domain of evil, as a Platonic cave of forgotten Paleolithic dreams. In Philip Pullman's *His Dark Materials* trilogy, religion tries to remove spirit animals or "dæmons" that are attached to the persons of children, hovering around them like witches' familiars. Patriarchal religion is precisely a device for excising the X-power of things and the way they are shadowed or haunted by futural versions of themselves that just won't stay still, dæmons that sit on your shoulder. And this is because patriarchal religion is a direct consequence of an even more efficient machine whose ruthless oblation of spectrality now goes by the name of the Sixth Mass Extinction Event. For the sake of lifeforms, it is time to release this seemingly evil spectral shimmering from its confinement in the realm of art and start allowing porpoises and humans to have it, too.

2

Specters

Yes, the whole world is haunted! Only is haunted? Nay, it itself "walks," it is uncanny through and through, it is the wandering seeming-body of a spirit, it is a spook.
— Max Stirner, *The Ego and Its Own*

Consider a phenomenon I shall call "correlationism revelation mode." My investigation will proceed in a psychoanalytic manner, by noting the inner pressure that seems to distort this mode: where does it come from?

There is a rhetorical pattern shared by descriptions of correlationism, aka post-Kantian philosophy and related cultural objects. It goes like this: "Boy oh boy will you ever be surprised when you find out that the object entails the subject! It will rock your world!" Even Kant works up a good head of steam about it, using the phrase "Unknown = X," as we just saw. This killer phrase evokes an approaching menace: you can't see it but it's real . . .! In Kant's case, the X turns out to be the transcendental subject, which seems attached to the human like a balloon.

Or, consider Heidegger. *Being and Time* is structured as a narrative reveal of Dasein: it slowly creeping up on the reader, boy oh boy is this going to be awesome . . .! Or Lacan. I have attended literary theory classes where the teacher makes a point of remarking, "Are you ever in for a surprise!" just before teaching his works. The surprise is that reality is a construct—amazing! Correlationism revelation mode appears very strongly in New Age literature. It often exclaims, "This is amazing, you never knew this before, but . . ." Consider for instance the tenor of the movie *What the Bleep Do We Know!?*[1]

From at least *The Tao of Physics* on, correlationism revelation mode has affected how we talk to one another about quantum theory.[2] Correlationism revelation mode appears in a whole array of cultural and literary criticism, Buddhist handbooks . . . it's everywhere. The "ideology of the aesthetic" works in the region of this mode. "Social space is fragmented but there is this thing, it glues everything back together, it's amazing! Saved!" There is an element of empowerment against crude reductionist materialism operating in each case. We seem not able to get enough of surprising ourselves with correlationism. It's like watching someone with hippocampus damage "waking up" again and again and again every five minutes, in a loop. Repeated over and over, it couldn't be more boringly conventional. One suspects that repetition is evidence of some unconscious aspect of what's going on: *I'm out of the loop! I'm out of the loop! I'm out of the loop! I'm* . . . It's oddly like Whiggish history, the kind that looks back at the past, say to the Roman Empire, and finds the bourgeoisie to be rising. Amazement and predictability weirdly overlap.

It has, in fact, been two centuries over which we've been telling ourselves that we're going to be amazed when we find that objects are blank screens for the purposes of (human) projection. Often, it's done in the mode of showing people they have *even more* power over nonhumans: "Once we used to manipulate extensional lumps, mostly by pushing them around mechanically. But now, check this out! We can *format* them before we even talk about manipulating them!" Correlationism revelation mode, no matter the intention of the discourse in which it appears, is a mode of sadistic enjoyment in which one can do anything to anything.

It's not what you think but *how* you think that is so often where the problem lies. Is it that people really don't know that *we've been telling ourselves this for two hundred years?* Is it that we want to reassure ourselves, over and over, just how manipulable things are, because the fact is that they aren't manipulable? Is there something about revelation mode that is *hardwired* into correlationism itself?

Or are we repeating surprise mode over and over because there is something *buried in the message* that we hope, in the back of our minds, repetition will reveal? Kant's thought is a repression-sublimation of what he knew about Mesmer and Swedenborg and animal magnetism. Animal magnetism is Mesmer's term for a force that surrounds and penetrates lifeforms and acts in a nonlocal, telekinetic, telepathic and hypnotic way on them to produce various effects. Obi Wan Kenobi describes it in *Star Wars*; the Nyae Nyae !Kung call it N!ow.[3] But what happens within correlationism is a privatization of this telekinetic force—it's as if you could reduce the Force to just one dot and put that dot firmly in the subject-object correlation. Religion melted in mid 1700s Europe and the "paranormal" leaked out; thinkers became fascinated, often trying to contain it or bowdlerize it. The historical sequence, then, is from animal magnetism to hypnotism to psychoanalytic transference. By the start of the twenty-first century, we arrive at mirror neurons. Thank god, there are extension lumps in that direction, too. Scientism breathes a sigh of relief, and so does correlationism. No need to worry about sounding like Yoda.

Kantian beauty is found in this anxious region. It's a bowdlerized version of telepathy or telekinesis, something like agency or liveliness emanating from something like an inanimate being, a painting or a piece of music. But it has been restricted to just one place in the universe (the interface between the artwork and the human subject), and restricted within that to a kind of "thinkfeel," the experience of reasoning as such (it's not useful or functional in any way). Can we hear Kant saying, "Wow, this is so amazing!" and another part of him saying, "This is *not* weird and sexy! I promise!" If he lets down his guard he's going to transmute into Yoda, and he half knows it.

It's as if the mode contradicts the message. We seem to be trying to hear something *profound* and *weird,* outside of Western philosophical space but somewhat contained in religion, "spirituality." Is it like repressed Paleolithic thought? A thought space that includes "spooky action at a distance"? It's embarrassing how easy it is to find it if one tries, and it's become evident that this is a key feature of physical causality.[4] If one de-privatizes correlationism, one arrives quickly at some idea that everything has agency, everything is "alive," possibly "conscious"; or that consciousness is just another mode of access among equal others, and so on. There is no need for surprise.

So, we churn over correlationism, detecting something in it, something whose repression actually *founds* it, such that it can structurally never talk about it. We churn it like churning stones trying to get butter out. Thus, the repetition is a symptom of something truly sad. We can't let ourselves go there. And, tragic irony: our very repetition enhances our sense of being able to manipulate. It is a form of Stockholm syndrome, whereby we reproduce the Severing by containing the correlationist explosion to just one, human part of the universe. Our excitement about it is a symptom that something is missing in the very content of traditional correlationism.

SPECTRAL PHENOMENOLOGY

What we encounter in the case of correlationism surprise mode is the specter of paranormal action. Distilled into its most basic form, what is haunting communism is the specter of spectrality itself. Why? Because spectrality is the flavor of the symbiotic real, where everything is what it is, yet nothing coincides exactly with itself. Communist thought needs to embrace the spectral and figure out exactly what comprises it: not spirits in a divine realm, even if that realm has been relocated in the human—that's the concept of Humanity. *Spectrality is nonhumans,* including the "nonhuman" aspects of ourselves. A convocation of specters will aid us in imagining something like an ecocommunism, a communism of humans and nonhumans alike.

"Specter" could mean "apparition," but it could also mean "horrifying object," or it could mean "illusion," or it could mean "the shadow of a thing."[5] The word "specter" is spectral by its own definition, wavering between appearance and being. In the specter, we encounter the ghostly presence of beings not yet formatted according to Nature, including the Nature in Marx: nonhumans subjected to human metabolism. Things in themselves haunt data: this is possibly the shortest way of describing the Continental philosophical tradition since Kant. Marx's version of it is that use-value is already on the human metabolic side of the equation: the spoon exists insofar as it becomes part of how I organize my enjoyment. It's what we hear in the fifteenth chapter of the first volume of *Capital*, with its imaginative architects and mechanical bees, namely, the sharp distinction between human being and everything else that Marx inherits from Kant, and in which Kant is still haunted by the specter of Descartes, namely that philosopher's substance ontology of purely extensional lumps connected mechanically.

The more we think ecological beings—a human, a tree, an ecosystem, a cloud—the more we find ourselves obliged to think them not as alive or dead, but as spectral. The more we think them, the more we discover that such beings are not solidly "real" nor completely "unreal"—in this sense, too, ecological beings are spectral. Since the difference between life and non-life is neither thin nor rigid, we discover that biology and evolution theory are actually telling us that we coexist *with* and *as* ghosts, specters, zombies, undead beings and other ambiguous entities, in a thick, fuzzy middle region excluded from traditional Western logic.

Marx distinguishes between humans and living nonhumans. Architects imagine and bees only execute, like computer programs. Unless we want humankind to be anthropocentric, we can't think like this. Marx also distinguishes between what capital does—it makes tables compute value—and what the paranormal does—it makes tables dance.[6] Capitalist tables are like artificial intelligence versions of the architect whereas paranormal tables are like spectral versions of the bee. Ironically, Marx is happier with capitalist tables than with tables that dance. Future communism must be a place where nonhumans such as frogs and bees can dance, and maybe even tables, too.

It simply cannot be proved, as Marx wants to, that the best of bees is never as good as the worst of (human) architects because the human uses imagination and the bee simply executes an algorithm.[7] Far more efficient than showing bees have the capacity of imagination (some science begins to move toward this possibility) is to show that it's impossible to prove that a human can. Prove that I'm not executing an algorithm when I seem to be planning something. Prove that asserting that humans do not blindly follow algorithms is not the effect of some blind algorithm. The most we can say is that human architects pass our Turing test for now, but that is no reason to say that they are in any sense better than bees. It is instead truer to assert that we are hamstrung as to determining whether humans are executions of algorithms or not, casting doubt on our certainty that bees really do only execute algorithms blindly, since that certainty is based on a metaphysical assertion about humans and is thus caught in fruitless circularity.

There are two possible reasons why I can't prove that I can imagine. Number one: there is no such thing as imagining at all; whatever we call "imagining" can be reduced to some material process. If this first were true, it would also drastically reduce reasons we have to care about lifeforms. An architect is just a deluded bee, and bees are just mechanisms. Number two: what is called "imagination" isn't directly present; it can't be pointed to straightforwardly; it has a spectral existence that includes a basic ontological uncertainty. On this view, a bee is a mislabeled architect.

In a world where it is hard to distinguish definitively between life and non-life, it is also hard to distinguish between bees and tables. Since we can't distinguish very rigidly between humans and bees, the difference between humans and tables shrinks. We are moving toward the object-oriented ontology view that all beings have agency, even mind. Significantly, we can glimpse this when Marx talks about Milton. This poet, second only to Shakespeare in the estimation of English literary history, acted like a silkworm when he wrote *Paradise Lost*. He didn't enter into a contract with a publisher in order for that publisher to make money. So, Milton was an "unproductive" worker because he didn't produce any surplus value.[8] Surplus value is produced when the capitalist obtains abstract homogeneous surplus labor time. Milton's auto-mated, nonhuman, algorithmic behavior—the poem just poured out of him—is valued, while the deliberate, "imaginative" entering into of a contract by a paid author is devalued. *Paradise Lost* was part of Milton the Silkworm's "extended phenotype," the expres-sion of his artistic genome, just as a beaver's genes don't end at its whiskers but at her or his dam.

This is an astounding reversal of the architect and the bee. It is the contract writer whose labor has been reduced upwards to an abstract, bland, homogeneous unit of labor time, so that it doesn't much matter what the writer is expressing. Marx uses "behave" (what bees do) in a positive sense in his notes on Adolph Wagner, in which he defines production differently than the commonly accepted notion, which seems to have much more to do with the *reified* production socialism is meant to oppose, rather like how we have confused time with the measurement of time:

> Men do not by any means begin by "finding themselves in this theo-retical relationship to the things of the outside world." They begin, like every animal, by eating, drinking, etc., that is not by "finding themselves" in a relationship, but actively behaving, availing them-selves of certain things of the outside world by action, and thus satis-fying their needs. (They start, then, with production.)[9]

Production is biting into a peach. Production is enjoyment, of one's biting and of the peach, of the nonhuman. Production is love, which includes sheer solidarity with the nonhuman—putting that peach right into your mouth and biting. Production is something you can't help doing. Production is a silkworm oozing out silk. And so, production is a bee building a hive. The appearance of the writing as such is sharply separated from the substance of writing as labor for profit. But in the case of Milton, the thing (the poet) and its appearance (the poem) are inextricable. There isn't a mind–body or substance–accidents dualism in operation here. And the dualism has vanished not through reductionism, not by saying that Milton is just a collection of subroutines, but by suggesting, if only in the imagery, that the spontaneously thingly, sensuous quality of Milton-who-can't-help-it is what emerges as a gorgeous poem. If only in the imagery, this softens the edges of the word "act" and sharpens the agency of the word "behave."

DANCING NONHUMANS

What was just said is in keeping with Marx's theory of commodity fetishism. Before we get into it, let's recall the opening paragraph of his explication in *Capital*:

> A commodity appears at first sight an extremely obvious, trivial thing. But its analysis brings out that it is a very strange thing, abounding in metaphysical subtleties and theological niceties. So far as it is a use-value, there is nothing mysterious about it, whether we consider it from the point of view that by its properties it satisfies human needs, or that it first takes on these properties as the product of human labour. It is absolutely clear that, by his activity, man changes the forms of the materials of nature in such a way as to make them useful to him. The form of wood, for instance, is altered if a table is made out of it. Nevertheless the table continues to be wood, an ordinary sensuous thing. But as soon as it emerges as a commodity, it changes into a thing that transcends sensuousness. It not only stands with its feet on the ground, but, in relation to all other commodities, it stands on its head, and evolves out of its wooden

brain grotesque ideas, far more wonderful than if it were to begin dancing of its own free will.[10]

Abstract homogeneous labor time is the goose that lays the golden eggs, that turns M (money) into M′ (more money) by passing through the commodity (C): the famous M–C–M′ formula. Capitalism acts like a drastic version of the default ontology of Western philosophy, reducing things to bland lumps of extension decorated with accidents. It doesn't matter whether or not I'm good at squeezing and you're good at hitting. Both actions are irrelevant to abstract labor time, and what they make is irrelevant to making money—whether a chocolate bar or a nuclear weapon. Thus, there is a transcendental gap between my actual labor and what I'm making (a use-value) and the commodity *form* (the format in which commodities come to determine value, in particular the value of abstract homogeneous labor time). As in Freud's idea that the secret wish is hidden in the format of a dream not in its manifest content, the secret of capitalism is hidden in the format of exchange value. "Commodity form" doesn't mean "the shape of this chocolate bar."

It doesn't matter what I'm creating or not creating, and it certainly doesn't matter what I feel or think about it. Specifically, it doesn't matter that I know that labor produces value—all capitalist theories know it, too. But it also doesn't matter that I know how commodity fetishism works—by computing the value of abstract labor time, so that chronologically my labor makes this chocolate bar, but logically the exchange value of the chocolate bar makes my labor time a commodity that I'm selling.

To hold that objects have agency, even simply to hold that they are thingly ("*dinglich*," Marx's own word in this passage in *Capital*), to think objects as sensuous, is not only irrelevant to capitalist operation, so that OOO definitely isn't a manifestation of commodity fetishism.[11] To hold that objects have agency is to resist the abstraction whereby the object becomes a mere blank screen for the computation of value, an extensional lump with a brain that "evolves" concepts rather like artificial intelligence. Thinking that tables can dance is *not* commodity fetishism. The commodity format is the exchange value structure in which abstract labor time is produced as a bland homogeneous lump, an extensional lump like a body, with a price on it like a mind that makes that body move around, as in Cartesian dualism. This is about as far from OOO as possible. Capitalism, if anything, is a metastasized form of idealism, in which just one nonhuman is allowed to have agency—a hyperobject. The hyperobject consists of homogeneous abstract labor time, abstracted from actual labor, which is a narrow bandwidth in the broader spectrum of production, namely creativity and its pleasures, including the sensation of biting into a peach and letting the juice run down your chin.

This all means that there is no good reason not to consider at least the sensuousness and specificity of nonhumans and the sensuousness and specificity of creativity. Commodity fetishism isn't about just the alienation of humans, but the alienation of any entity whatsoever from its sensuous qualities, as we just saw. Production, as in the writing of a brilliant poem, is the thing you can't help doing, your species-being. This is exactly how it can be exploited. It just happens anyway, so that the capitalist can dip a bucket into its flow to extract labor time from it and homogenize it. The capitalist exploits this fact, the non-chosen, non-"imaginative" part of me that I don't have to plan, the fact that I'm a being like a silkworm. Which is precisely why my labor can be equated with the productivity of the soil—both are conveniently spontaneous bits of "nature" that capitalism can turn into blank screens for value computation.

This spontaneous part of myself tyrannizes me as if it were an external being—this is alienation. It is as if capitalism has forced a bionic soul into my poor helpless body, animating it like a Cartesian zombie. Now, its sensuality and specific creativity are just veils. This is the true horror of capitalism: it turns me not into an object but into a parody of a person, an anthropocentric machine with a soul, as in Descartes or Aristotle; and that soul isn't mine. No wonder

Aimé Césaire proclaimed that he was for "proletarianization and mystification."[12] Demystification, rudely stripping the appearance from things and laying them bare, is the capitalist operation par excellence. I am pouring chocolate into a mold in just this precise way. Neither me nor the chocolate nor the mold are exhausted by the ways in which we mutually access one another. At the same time, homogeneous abstract labor time is being siphoned off. Even if I'm not suffering terribly, I have been exploited, as in alien abduction.

The nonhuman aspect of humans, the fact that *production is how they behave*, is exactly what capitalism exploits, along with other nonhumans such as the microbes in the soil. In a strong sense, Marxism already includes nonhumans! And this is where we touch the symbiotic real, because species-being implies symbiosis. Capital is anthropocentric and this is precisely how it messes with humankind, human species-being as a part of the symbiotic real. The part of the human that has a foot in the nonhuman. Like phenomenological style, of which ego is at best a very thin and distorted slice, *the nonhuman aspect of the human* is precisely what is spoken in the word "humankind."[13] Kindred, friendship, solidarity, symbiosis—this kind-ness is spoken here.

The Enlightenment idea of vanilla mankind and its postmodern flip side, the not-all set of incommensurable differences, are both reflexes of capital. Both are anthropocentric. Both distort humankind. Un-distortion of humankind requires amplifying the nonhuman symbiotic real implied in the concept of species-being. So, what happens when we turn up the volume of the nonhumans within Marxism?

No longer able to exclude nonhumans with a straight face, thought is confronted with its anthropocentrism. Bees and architects are important because for Marx, in the lineage of Kant, there is a Decider that makes things real. For Marx, the Decider is human economic relations. But ecological relations subtend human relations of all kinds, and ecological relations extend beyond them throughout the biosphere. Humans can organize their enjoyment (economics) because they participate in the symbiotic real.

Human economic relations are simply general ecological relations with arbitrary pieces missing—colossal numbers of pieces. Either Marxism can be thought in a way that includes this irreversible knowledge, or it cannot. If it can, then communism must involve greater and better relations with nonhumans than the ones in play right now. As Marx says in the chapter on machines in *Capital*, capitalism produces the misery of the worker and the depletion of the soil:

> All progress in capitalist agriculture is a progress in the art, not only of robbing the worker, but of robbing the soil; all progress in increasing the fertility of the soil for a given time is a progress towards ruining the more long-lasting sources of that fertility ... Capitalist production, therefore, only develops the techniques and the degree of combination of the social process of production by simultaneously undermining the original sources of all wealth—the soil and the worker.[14]

Soil is decomposing life forms and the bacteria whose extended phenotype these life forms are.[15] Marx implies nonhumans, yet he erases them—it's the *fertility* of the soil whose loss he laments, and this fertility is keyed to human metabolism; the soil is seen as it is accessed by humans. This is anthropocentric soil. But the good news is that the implication of nonhumans means that we might be able to un-erase them within Marxism; such an action seems highly unlikely within the realm of strict capitalist economic theory.

What is called Nature is a way to blind and deafen oneself to the strangeness of the symbiotic real. Ecological awareness, just now occurring to everyone on Earth, is a way to take one's hands away from one's ears, to hear a message that was transmitted loud and clear in the later eighteenth century, a message that not even its messengers wanted entirely to hear.

Kant blocked his ears to the implications of his correlationism, that nonhumans could also be correlators and not just correlatees.

Kant limited the gap he had discovered to the gap between human beings and everything else. It is time to release the copyright control on this gap. The name of this release is ecological awareness. Ecological awareness is coexisting, in thought and in practice, with the ghostly host of nonhumans. Thinking, itself, is one modality of the convocation of specters in the symbiotic real. To this extent, one's "inner space" is a test tube for imagining a being-with that our metaphysical rigidity refuses to imagine, like a quaking peasant with a string of garlic, warding off the vampires.

This would not necessarily be a bizarre stretch. Recall that commodity fetishism means that a table, a piece of fruit, a cloud of carbon dioxide, begin to operate like computer programs, chattering with one another about their exchange value as if a coat could become a screen on which were projected the fluctuations of value. The point is that turning tables into platforms for something like an artificial intelligence algorithm that computes exchange value is *far stranger* than if we accepted that tables could act in a paranormal way, which is to say, a "magical" way outside of normative modernity, by dancing around of their own accord, or telekinetically. That is precisely what Marx says about commodity fetishism: dancing tables are less weird than computing tables.

The future thought that Marx is unable quite to articulate himself is right there, not exactly in the argument but in the imagery. This future thought is strangely rather easy to decipher. In commodity fetishism, spoons and chickens do not have agency: they become the hardware platform for capitalist software. It is far *easier* than that to allow for the dancing tables of Marx, let alone dancing chimpanzees. We are not erasing the sensuousness of such beings in so doing. It is not that capitalism flirts with the spectral but that *capitalism is not spectral enough*. Capitalism implies a substance ontology that sharply divides what things are—"normal" or "natural" fixed essences (extensional lumps without qualities)— from how things appear, defanging and demystifying the things, stripping them of qualities and erasing their data. Imagine an ecological future.[16] This requires accepting that some forms of mystery are good: "They talk to me about civilization, I talk about proletarianization and mystification" (Aimé Césaire).[17]

THE SPECTRAL CHEMISTRY OF ECOLOGICAL ATTUNEMENT

The phenomenology of encountering an ecological being—how the encounter unfolds—will give us clues for thinking the spectrality of lifeforms. Meeting an ecological being is a moment at which I encounter something that is not me such that even if this being is obviously part of me—say, my brain—I don't experience it as part of the supposed whole that makes up "me." Ecological thought is Adorno's ideal of thinking as the encounter with non-identity.[18] When it isn't simply pushing preformatted pieces around, thought meets specters, which is to say, beings whose ontological status is profoundly and irreducibly ambiguous.

To encounter an ecological entity is to be *haunted*. Something is already there, before I think it. When we talk about haunting, what we are talking about is what phenomenology calls givenness. Givenness is the condition of possibility for data (in Latin, "what is given"). There is already a light in the refrigerator before I open the door to see whether or not the light is on. The light's givenness—it's a light, not an octopus—is not something I have planned, predicted or formatted. I cannot reduce this givenness to something expected, predictable, planned, without omitting some vital element of givenness as such. Givenness is therefore always surprising, and surprising in surprising ways: *surprisingly surprising*. Yet in haunting, the phenomenon of the disturbing, surprising given whose surprise cannot be reduced, also repeats itself.

Each time givenness repeats there is no lessening of surprise. Repetition leads not to boredom but to an uncanny sense of refreshment. It is as if I'm tasting something familiar yet slightly disgusting, as if I were to find, upon putting it to my lips, that my favorite drink had mold on its surface. I am stimulated by the very repetition itself: stimulated by boredom. Another term for this is ennui. Ennui is the quintessence of the consumerist experience: I'm stimulated by the boredom of being constantly stimulated. In ennui I heighten the Kantian window shopping of the bohemian or Romantic consumer.

The experience of vicarious experience—wondering what it would be like to be the person who wears *that* shirt—itself becomes too familiar, slightly disgusting, distasteful. I can't enjoy it "properly": I'm unable to achieve the familiar aesthetic distance from which to appreciate it as beautiful (or not). Disgust is the flip side of good taste in this respect: good taste is the ability to be appropriately disgusted by things that are in bad taste. I have had too many vicarious thrills, and now I find them slightly disgusting— but not disgusting enough to turn away from them altogether. I enjoy, a little bit, this disgust. This is ennui.

Since in an ecological age there is no appropriate scale on which to judge things (human? microbe? biosphere? DNA?), there can be no pure, unadulterated, totally tasteful beauty. Beauty is always a little bit weird, a little bit disgusting. Beauty always has a slightly nauseous taste of the kitsch about it, kitsch being the disgusting enjoyment object of the other, disgusting precisely because it is the other's enjoyment-thing, and thus inexplicable to me. Moreover, since beauty is an enjoyment that hasn't to do with my ego and is thus a not-me, beauty is always haunted by its spectral double, the kitsch. The kitsch precisely is the other's enjoyment object: how can anyone in their right mind want to buy this snow globe of the Mona Lisa? Yet there they are, hundreds of them, in this tourist shop.

Since beauty involves me in organizing enjoyment, it is a profoundly *economic* phenomenon in the interesting sense that its use-value has not yet been determined.[19] Beauty provides a way to think economics that crosses over the correlationist boundary between things and data, between what things are and how things appear. Beauty provides a channel through which nonhuman specters can enter. They do not have to be left out in the prefabricated "nature" of bourgeois ideology.

Rather than abolishing beauty, we can remix it for our own purposes. Beauty is always a love letter from an unknown source, a nonlocal telepathic mind-meld with something that might not be conscious, might not be sentient, might not be alive, might not even exist . . . beauty is a feeling of unconditional solidarity with things, with everything, with anything. Beauty is the nonhuman footprint of a nonhuman—a not-me experience arising in my inner space that bears the trace of a specter. And ennui is when we allow beauty to begin to lose its anthropocentric equalization. In ennui I am not totally turning my back on this sickening world; where would I turn to anyway, since the ecological world is the symbiotic real? Ennui is the correct ecological attunement!

The pathway to nonhumans is through a trapdoor in the ideological superstructure of capitalism, which is exactly why it seems so unacceptable. The very consumerism that haunts environmentalism—the consumerism that environmentalism explicitly opposes and finds disgusting—provides the model for how ecological awareness should proceed. Moreover, this ecological awareness would not depend on the "right" or "proper" ecological being, and thus would not depend on a metaphysical pseudo-fact. Consumerism is the specter of ecology. Ecological awareness must embrace its specter.

In ennui I find myself surrounded and penetrated by entities that I can't shake off. When I try to shake one off, another one attaches or I find another one is already attached, or that the very attempt to shake it off makes it tighten the grip of its suckers. Isn't this just the quintessence of ecological awareness, namely the feeling that I am surrounded and penetrated by entities such as stomach bacteria, parasites, mitochondria—not to mention other humans, lemurs and sea foam? I find it slightly disgusting and yet fascinating. I am "bored" in the sense that I find it provocative to include all the beings that I try to ignore in my awareness all the time. Who hasn't become "bored" in this way by ecological discourse? And who really wants to know that in a world where there is no "away" to flush our toilet waste to, it phenomenologically sticks to us, even after we have flushed it?

Isn't this abjection experience part of the phenomenology of what Marx calls species-being, when we consider it with an emphasis on the accessee, rather than the accessor? Consider the *Economic and Philosophical Manuscripts*:

> Nature is the inorganic body of a man . . . in so far as it is not itself a human body. That man lives from nature means that nature is his body with which he must maintain a constant interchange so as not to die. That man's physical and intellectual life depends on nature merely means that nature depends on itself, for man is a part of nature.[20]

If we invert the image of what Marx thinks as human "universality," we obtain exactly the abject awareness that I can't peel nonhumans from me without ceasing to be myself. There is no way to be a fully formed Hegelian subject, since this would involve sloughing off the nonhumans ("nature" in the passage above) that are my "inorganic body." I am a way in which "nature depends on itself"— an elegant paraphrase of "symbiotic real." I exist as a part of this symbiotic real that is human (and nonhuman) species-being. Within a single page, Marx does go on to say that I differ from nonhumans in my ability to change how I participate in symbiosis, which provides the basis for the strong correlationist interpretation that unlike nonhumans, human species-being is the way in which humans create their own environment, an idea so caught in Hegelian antics that it forgets the simple fact of termites or beavers and any kind of "extended phenotype," the fact that a spider's genome includes not only spider legs but also spiders' webs.[21]

Let's continue exploring the phenomenology of the symbiotic real. Consider the *Paris Spleen* poems of Charles Baudelaire, poet-consumerist par excellence, bohemian inventor of the *flâneur*, or rather, the one who christened this quintessential, "Kantian" mode of consumption; the poet who originated the notion of ennui. One should read the poems in their entirety for various reasons. First, there is a general structure of feeling across the poems. Second, the provocative titling—exactly the same ("Spleen") for four poems in sequence in *The Flowers of Evil*—compels us to read them together, as if the same affect were collapsing, or going to sleep, then queasily restarting each time. Third, this format suggests being haunted, in the sense of being frequented, of an event occurring more than once. We all know there would be no such thing as the uncanny without the notion of repetition. Space permits me only to quote one of these poems:

The month of drizzle, the whole town annoying, a dark cold pours from its urn in torrents on the pale inhabitants of the adjoining cemetery and over the mortals in foggy suburbs.

My cat, looking for a tile to sleep on, fidgets restlessly his thin mangy body; the soul of some old poet trundles down the rainspout with the sad voice of a chilly phantom.

A bumblebee moans, the smoking log backs up in falsetto the congested clock; meanwhile in a game reeking with sordid perfumes—

Mortal descent from an old dropsical dame—the handsome jack of hearts and the queen of spades make sinister small talk about their defunct loves.[22]

All kinds of incongruous things blend together, even the difference between consumerism and ecological awareness. Living and dead things become confused and weigh on the narrator, depressing him. Ecological awareness interrupts my anthropocentric mania to think myself otherwise than being surrounded and permeated with other beings, not to mention made up of them? Which is to say, isn't ecological awareness a spectrality that consists of awareness of specters? One is unsure whether a specter is material or illusory, visible or invisible. What weighs on Baudelaire is the specter of his bohemian, Romantic consumerism, his Kantian floating, enjoyment tinged with disgust tinged with enjoyment. Ennui is being surrounded by the spectral presence of evacuated enjoyment.

Somewhere within consumerist possibility space, between defiant rejection (like punk) and perverse acceptance (like pop art), resides this Baudelairean structure of feeling, and it might be very useful for imagining the location of the trapdoor toward the symbiotic realm. You can't get out through rejection, because the skylight is always within consumerist space: we enter the endless dialectic of authentic versus sell-out. You can't get out through perverse acceptance either, although this is more promising than rejection: rejection is (because of the paradox I just outlined) a form of acceptance-in-denial. Something like uneasy acceptance of disgust, disgusted acceptance of unease, accepting disgust at ambiguity, accepting ambiguous feelings about disgust . . . these provide the chemicals that might melt the floor and allow a way through to the symbiotic real and its solidarity hum, a way we locate *underneath* consumerist possibility space.

When thinking becomes ecological, the beings it encounters cannot be established in advance as living or non-living, sentient or non-sentient, real or epiphenomenal. Biology is founded on this confusion. What we encounter when we access the symbiotic real are spectral beings whose ontological status is uncertain to the extent that we know them in detail as we never have before. Our experience of these spectral beings is itself spectral, just like ennui. Starting the engine of one's car isn't what it used to be, since one knows one is releasing greenhouse gases. Eating a fish means eating mercury and depleting a fragile ecosystem. Not eating a fish means eating vegetables, which may have relied on pesticides and other harmful agricultural logistics. Because of interconnectedness, it always feels as if there is a piece missing. Something just doesn't add up, in a disturbing way. We are never clear of embodiment. We can never achieve cynical escape velocity. We are caught in hypocrisy. We can't get compassion exactly right. Being nice to bunny rabbits means not being nice to bunny rabbit predators. Giving up in sophisticated boredom is also an oppressive option.

The spectral beings that compose the symbiotic real are disclosed as *partial objects*. These are parts of a whole that they exceed. Are we dealing with a violation of logic that then forms the basis for turning the ontological camera the other way, and attributing this partiality of the object to (human) fantasy, namely the Freudian version of the correlationist Decider? How we think wholes needs to change: what happens if we take another pathway than reducing objects to the Decider? Perhaps the idea of the partial object is a by-product of a certain set theory, a certain theory about wholes. Perhaps if we changed the meaning of holism, partial objects would be partial on their own, from their own side, not because (human) desire projected a fantasy onto what was essentially a blank screen, even more useless than a mere lump of extended stuff to be manipulated by the human.

God is the being that gets to avoid being a partial object. That should give us a clue as to the origin of the holism that enables this thought in agricultural society, otherwise known as the Neolithic. Explosive holism is born here. So, what we are aiming for must be an *implosive holism*. According to such a holism, a being such as God wouldn't matter. We wouldn't need to prove or disprove God's existence; that would be cognitively inefficient. Far more efficient would be to imagine that if there were a god of some kind, that god couldn't be omnipresent or omniscient because it couldn't be constantly present, because such a being wouldn't comprise a whole of which we are the components. In explosive holism, the parts are reducible to the whole. We all know what comes next: "As flies to wanton boys are we to the gods, / They kill us for their sport."[23] We are insignificant, because God is more . . . *there*.

Hieronymus Bosch depicts hell as a space of obscene enjoyment and horror, the space of partial objects (stomach, buttocks), and a space of symbiosis (birds excreting humans). This is an organicism, but not explosively holist organicism, which is a form of mechanism (Greek "*organon*," tool or machine). We could call it *anorganic form*, to distinguish from the organic, and its opposite, the inorganic. Or consider the meme about First Peoples' beliefs on being photographed—that to be photographed is to have your "soul" stolen. Isn't this precisely because the photograph reveals your spectrality? I cannot think myself as "inside here" any more; I'm decisively "over there" in some way; my being is not organically locked together; my "soul" can be detached from other parts of me. Anyone who has experienced the uncanny sound of her or his voice on tape, or investigated the fascination with hearing ghosts on tape or seeing them in photographs, or who has seen their face from the side in a film, has an idea about this kind of partial being.

Explosive holism is part of Marx's theory of capitalism. Industrial capitalism, the truest face of capitalism, is an emergent property of enough machines making enough machines, linked together in a complex-enough network.[24] Capitalism for Marx is another version of the invisible sadist who wants to kill you.

The trouble is, such an idea is itself an example of the very ideological displacement Feuerbach and Marx want to invert: human powers displaced onto a transcendental superbeing. These powers are best thought of not as exclusively human individual powers, but as transpersonal and even trans-species powers, since the lionization of the exclusively human inherent in this concept of ideology is itself an artifact of the Severing. These are powers inherent in the symbiotic real, which Marx recognizes as an extension of the human body, if not of nonhuman bodies. Feuerbach argued that religious statements such as "God is love" are alienated expressions of human powers ("Love is god"). Debugged Feuerbachian ideology theory would proclaim that the seemingly paranormal superpowers displaced onto an explosively holist superbeing are common to all lifeforms, and, since there is no convenient way to contain the concept of non-life within a thin, rigid boundary, to all beings whatsoever.

X-EXISTENCE

We are in fact living in an age of mass extinction, the sixth one on this planet so far—"so far" meaning the roughly four-and-a-half-billion-year history of life on Earth. There have been five others previously: the Ordovician-Silurian mass extinction; the late Devonian mass extinction; the Permian mass extinction; the Triassic-Jurassic mass extinction; and the Cretaceous-Tertiary mass extinction. The objective content of the Anthropocene is the gigantic die-off of lifeforms, as all are sucked in some sense or other into the one-size-fits-all, narrow-diameter temporality pipe of agrilogistics, a program that is still running.

This mass extinction is invisible. It's the most significant moment for lifeforms on this planet since the dinosaurs got wiped by that asteroid, and we can't see it directly—we see only spatiotemporal pieces of it. *We are the asteroid.* Popular stories about "the world without us" or movies such as *Melancholia* disturbingly displace that fact. An apocalyptic disaster (literally a malfunctioning star) isn't coming from outer space to kill us. It's us. A gamma ray burst within six thousand light years can cause a mass extinction. A gigantic surge of methane from the ocean floor triggered by global warming, known as a clathrate gun, caused what we call the End Permian extinction, otherwise known as the Great Dying: all life on Earth right now is descended from the 4 percent that survived that one. And this time, *we* are the explosive force. And we can't see it; even scientists find it very difficult to point to. What is disturbing is that the hyperobject has the hallmarks of the forms of entity humans made up early in the agricultural age, the gods of the Axial Age religions. Only, it's not conveniently located in some beyond only accessible by some top-level human with exclusive access, like the king or whoever, and handily capable of taking my mind off my daily misery. The hyperobject is in my genome, it's on my oily fingers, it's in the sound of my starter motor. It's under my skin and it is my skin. I myself am a tiny crystal on an asteroid.

I confront something like what Kant was calling the Unknown = X: a beautiful, uncanny term for how there must be this transcendental dimension that gives meaning to the empirical one we can experience. I only glimpse it anamorphically, like that skull rotated into a dimension at ninety degrees to the illusionist 3-D space of Holbein's *Ambassadors* painting. The Sixth Mass Extinction and humankind are a gigantic shadow and the executant entity of which it's a gigantic shadow. An individual fish dying isn't quite it; a fish species dying out isn't quite it. Me turning the ignition of my car isn't quite it: that action alone is statistically meaningless. But when you scale these things up, suddenly—and it's sudden, a quantum jump rather than a smooth transition—this gigantic entity emerges. It was there all along, but I was inside it and I was it, and it's uncannily dislocated from my empirical experiences and effects in the world. I don't mean to harm Earth, and in fact *I'm not harming Earth*. My action is statistically meaningless. But billions of things such as key turnings in ignitions are exactly what is causing global warming and mass extinction. I'm good at seeing my cat and my car as entities because they are anthropocentrically scaled: I can grasp them both figuratively and literally. What's ironic is that the actual human species, the anthropo- part that some of us are too uncomfortable for various reasons even to name, is the thing I can't see! To put it in Marxian, the Anthropocene is where I get to glimpse my species-being as a power stands over against me, as when in a club strangely called Earth in 1989 I experienced a rain of human sweat that had accumulated on the ceiling after hours and hours of techno. Parts of everyone were falling, alien, damp, warm, back onto everyone, because of our own repetitive churning.

The uncanny spectrality of mass extinction: colossal, but you can't point to it directly. Furthermore, we're talking here about *future traces*, so they are spectral in that sense too—they haven't all appeared yet, these traces of beings. This poses a scientific problem. How to find patterns in data that show you that mass extinction is happening is causing scientists to use the language of spectrality. Spectrality itself is the signal and it has an empirical signature, like ectoplasm, in the form of "species rarity": just a few of a certain kind of fish swimming around down there for some reason, oddly too few.[25] It's like looking at de Chirico's *Mystery and Melancholy of a Street*: a girl reduced to silhouette rolls a hoop across an empty street that stretches into the far distance. It's quiet, too quiet—but it's not silent. It's easier to look at slices of rock, core samples from millions of years ago, geological strata that tell you of these absences, conveniently wedged and compacted and foreshortened, than it is to detect the current one, the Sixth Mass Extinction Event. They are nicely present-at-hand, as Heidegger would say, their inconsistencies jut out of the geologic contexture. The other five big mass extinctions are *vorhanden*. But this one is what Heidegger would call ready-to-hand, *zuhanden*, because it is part of our human world, our projects, such as taking a flight.

Moreover, the specific project of agrilogistics is precisely a severing of human–nonhuman ties that *enables* a human confrontation with a seemingly smoothly functioning world—even Heidegger himself thinks that this smooth functioning is itself smoothly functioning. Sealed off from other beings, the concept of world becomes vacuum-sealed and shrink-wrapped. Object-oriented ontology tries to go one level deeper within Heideggerian thought, into the realm of entities that are never exhausted by access at all; not that they last forever, but that they are mysterious or open or unspeakable in some sense. This must mean that worlds are never capable of being smooth, because they always imply gaps between the reality of the entity doing the accessing on the one hand, and the symbiotic real on the other.

The smoothly functioning human world is now malfunctioning precisely because of this gap between our world, with its anthropocentric access modes, and actual reality. And—this is the uncanny part—there we are, woven into the coral reef of actual entities underneath the smoothly gliding submarine of human civilization—*we are one of those unspeakable entities*! We, as humankind—not as in some racist or speciesist fantasy, which is precisely invented to allow us to believe we can point out what a human being is, in the sense of distinguishing the human from the nonhuman or the inhuman in some rigid way. Human species-being oozes into human awareness. We are the asteroid, which is to say that the gap between the human world and the human species is exactly the cause of the spectrality I'm talking about. It's also to say that, so far, industrial economic relations between humans, relations based on property (private or state), have had asteroid-like impacts on Earth.

Our world is now malfunctioning sufficiently for us to begin to glimpse the darker, weirder malfunctioning—the sinister *mal* that might be intrinsic to functioning as such. Spectrality is the *mal* of this functioning, not just a superficial appearance, but exactly the sound of extinction faintly audible behind the din of the motor-cars, its incredible weakness a horrible symptom of its colossal power. And the humanists, the art historians, the literary scholars, the music scholars, the philosophers, the historians, *we know this! We know what it is. We've been studying this for years, just exactly and precisely this.*

To do speculative realism, to do ecological criticism, you don't need to jump to some incredibly different domain with incredibly different vocabulary. You can use what you have. You just need to relax that anthropocentric reference frame, doesn't even have to be all the way, just like you don't have to *completely* remove the boron rods from a nuclear reactor for something interesting to happen. You just have to let a little bit of the explosion we've been trying to contain happen, the explosion we've been trying to contain for about two centuries, for as long as the time of industrial fossil fuel burning so far. It started with the steam engine, the general-purpose machine noted by Marx as a vital component of industrial capitalism, and by Paul Crutzen as the instigator of what is now called the Anthropocene.[26]

It really shouldn't be surprising to humanist scholars that to see data patterns about entities such as extinction at the right ontological level, you need to look at specters themselves, like studying poetry: the processes operating on you, the reader, are hiding in plain sight in the flickering of language. Normal, old New Leftish scholars of the world, unite! You have nothing to lose but your anthropocentrism! Come on in, the water's lovely, which is to say, it's cold and dark and mysterious and spooky.

Spectrality has become the tool with which the pattern is to be found. Pincelli Hull refers to spectrality as a signal of mass extinction: "The researchers note, that the modern ocean is full of ecological 'ghosts'—species that are now so rare that they no longer fill the ecological roles they did previously, when they were more abundant. Species rarity itself, rather than extinction, can lead to a cascade of changes within ecosystems, long before the species goes extinct, the scientists explain." Or: "The ecological ghosts of oceans past already swim in emptied seas."[27]

Spectrality isn't just an ineffectual aesthetic flicker on top of a mechanical bumping about of flavorless reality cakes. Spectrality is a very precise ontological category, not just a haze that makes anything metaphysical impossible.

Darwin argues that at every step of evolution there is mutation. Things don't evolve teleologically. DNA mutation is random with respect to current need. We know this. But can we *imagine* it, as Shelley might say? What does it actually mean?

It means something quite amazing.

Stop the tape of evolution at any point and you will find a species, shadowed by some X-power. A fish that can leap out of water and survive for more than a few seconds by gulping air, let's say. There seems to be no point to this flamboyant behavior. Some fish might find it disturbing, even insulting to fish-kind. Perhaps this fish is dangerous. Perhaps it needs to be confined or put on drugs for its own good; it might do itself harm. The fish is indeed dangerous: *ontologically* dangerous. Dangerous to the fish who think that they have "I am exactly this fish" inscribed all the way through every part of their structure.

Just in the same way as Irigaray talks about sexuality, a species isn't one and it isn't two.[28] What is the case is a species shadowed by an X-species. Parrots and X-parrots. Men and X-men. Women and X-women. Live oaks and X–live oaks. Cyanobacteria and X-cyanobacteria, which have the special ability to live inside other single-celled organisms: these X-cyanobacteria are called *chloroplasts* and they are why plants are green and can photosynthesize. Likewise, some anaerobic bacteria hid in differently-evolving single celled organisms, and now you have them in every cell of your body. They are called *mitochondria* and they are why you are capable of reading this: they provide your energy. Your eyes are moving down this page because of a bacterial superpower.

You can't be a lifeform unless you have this spectral double, this mutant shadow. Being alive means being supernatural.

A species is not an individual. I can subdivide it into its members, and there are future and past versions of it. But it's not individual, in a much more profound, structural sense. Species is not individual because it can't be counted as a "one": a species is haunted by its X-species *in order to exist at all.* In this sense, a species is utterly *unique*—because this "one-plus-X" quality is ungraspable, because a mutation isn't "for" anything, because it's unpredictable in a strong sense. There is a vivid difference between being individual and being unique. Just ask a standard garden lawn, a classic American expression of individualism; and then consult a lawn covered in psychedelic crucifixes and "outsider" art, an expression of uniqueness that is often illegal.

This is the deep way in which the concept of humankind isn't about putting beings into preformatted boxes at all. It's not just that right now my human identity is scooped out by some future existence as a post-human being. All we are doing in that case is just replacing a metaphysics of separated self-identical humans with a metaphysics of a self-identical flow of matter or life, of which I and my mutated future version are just instances. The net effect on the problem of reifying species is nil.

What is in fact the case is that right now, at this very moment, my existence is always already shadowed by my X-existence, as a condition of possibility for my existing at all. It isn't that frogs and humans and cyanobacteria are not really real, while some underlying flow of "life" is. There *are* frogs and they *aren't* octopuses; they are irreducible. But there are only frogs on condition that every frog has, as its shadow, its X-frog doppelganger. The monotheistic concept of soul and body is a way of domesticating this spookiness, tying it down to a non-migrant hierarchical social structure. The soul sits nicely in the body, and it isn't the body. The X-frog floats uneasily around the frog, and it *is* the frog—and it *isn't*, at the same time. As Freud observes in his essay on the uncanny, the concept of *soul* is shadowed by the concept of *specter*.[29] Ecological awareness is saturated with *nothingness*, a shimmering or flickering, a shadow play of presence and absence intertwined. What does this feel like from moment to moment?

Time isn't like that either. Because of what I've just argued, time itself is not a line of reified atomic now-points, but a spooky shifting that haunts itself, slightly in front or behind itself, the rippling play of light and shadow in the pond water reflected on the underside of a sundial on a late summer afternoon, a vibrant stillness that is far from static. The present is haunted by the X-present. I call this manifold of present and X-present "nowness," a shifting, haunted region like evaporating mist, a region that can't be tied to a specific timescale.

Nowness is a dynamic relation between the past and the future. According to the spectral logic I'm outlining, the present isn't present! It doesn't exist, at least not like that. The belief that "animals" are superior or inferior to humans because they live in an eternal now is untrue, because no being lives in a now. This is what is wrong with the second foot of Marx's species-being, the foot in anthropocentrism. Furthermore, past and future are artifacts of the structure of entities as such, and are to be found nowhere outside of them. The form of a thing, its appearance, is the *past*. My face is a map of everything that happened to my face. A beehive is a story about what happened when some bees chewed some wax. There is a contextual abyss about appearance: we can't draw the line decisively as to when the face stops and its explanatory context—all the things that happened to give it this exact appearance—begins. This provides the basis for the "nightmare" quality of past states of humankind that weigh on us: there might be no end to the "weight of dead traditions."[30]

On the other hand, the essence of a thing, its being, is the *future*. Entities are not entirely caught like algorithms in the gravitational pull of the past. There is also *levity*: the lightness of futurality. The future is also an abyss. What will happen to my face next? I'm unsure, not just because it's hard to predict at least somewhat far into the measureable future, but for the deeper reason that the measurable future depends on an infinite (uncount-able) futurality, the withdrawal-quality of a thing, so that what-ever access mode I use (thinking-about, dabbing-lotion-on, photographing-a-selfie-of), my face slips away like a liquid. The one place our ultra-utilitarian culture has cordoned off as a zone in which this kind of thing is barely tolerated is called *art*. But in truth, everything behaves like that. Everything is a railway junc-tion where past and future are sliding over one another, not touching.

We will revisit this idea frequently: appearance is the past; being is the future; nowness is the relative motion of future over past, not touching. A thing is a junction of two abyssal movements. Solidarity is the noise the symbiotic real makes in its floating, spectral nowness, conditioned by the past (otherwise known as trauma), yet open to the future. Creativity and enjoyment are a "disabled," malfunctioning relative motion between past and future, appear-ance and being.

X-existence happens in the symbiotic real because the ontologi-cal structure of a thing allows it. To exist is to X-exist. You can't be counted as one. But you also can't be counted as two. Your spectral double is *your* spectral double, not some frog's. But it isn't proper to you. It's highly improper, in fact; it violates every notion of property and propriety. It's indecent of fish to breathe air. The manifold of species and X-species is fractal; it lies somewhere between one and two, and the logic of this in-between area must be *modal*: it must violate strict versions of the Law of the Excluded Middle, so that things can be sort of true, kind of real, slightly wrong. It is as if every indicative sentence is shadowed by its subjunctive double, the sentence in "perhaps" mode. The sentence is open. It isn't nothing, and it isn't exactly something. Meaning as such is its spectral shadow. Who knows what a poem is really saying? But this poem is *this* poem, not *that* poem.

ACTING AND BEHAVING, FUTURE AND PAST

In a non-metaphysical, which is to say post-Kantian, sense, we cannot rely on a *teleological* concept of species-being, a definition of the human based on an anthropocentric metaphysics that distinguishes the human architect who *acts* from the bee that (and I suspect the neuter would be the preferred pronoun here) *behaves*. We need to peel away the second page of Marx's description of species-being in *Economic and Philosophical Manuscripts* from the first page.

This is urgent, not superficial. If a bee only behaves, and if a bee is a worker, a robot (from the Czech term for "worker"), then the bee is already as if alienated in a capitalist structure, one which doesn't even need human input, but which spreads throughout the symbiotic real, reified as Nature: "the way things are," which is to say, how they predictably *behave*. This is capitalist realism applied to nonhumans. It's a bug, not a feature, of Marxism. The bee is permanently caught in the past, because if it only executes an algorithm, it's executing some past state of the bee genome. So, not only is Nature mechanical and reified (no matter how squishy and green it looks), Nature is also frozen in the past. But if human species-being, which is a part of the symbiotic real, is frozen in the past, there is no way for it to be creative. Workers, by implication, are caught forever in a naturalized capitalist state! It's the past to the power of two, as a matter of fact, because the automated labor they perform must represent a past state of social requirements. I'm pretty sure this entrapment of workers in the past isn't what Marx really wanted.

On the other hand, acting seems entirely futural. To act is to be like the capitalist, mastering time by projecting a future in which M will have transformed into M-prime. The absolute, I-can-do-anything-to-anything Kantian freedom of the capitalist is hard-wired into this picture of human labor! Acting is imprisoned in the future, which means that any attempt to transform humankind's enjoyment modes into communist modes will only be utopian, never arriving. And to work is to be a boss: only the capitalist really does it. I'm sure Marx didn't mean *that*, either.

The sharp difference between "to act" and "to behave" expresses a class division that is structural to capitalism. And it expresses a severing of the nonhuman (the algorithmic, the past) from the human (the imaginative, the future). That, as they say, totally sucks.

It seems necessary to soften the edges between "act" and "behave" if we are going to create a communist theory of action. "To act" and "to behave" need to be seen as dual aspects of one being. They slide over one another, generating a spectral, breathing nowness. This nowness is open and so it is capable of novelty, or as Marx says, the poetry of the future.[31] Nowness is the mode in which solidarity appears. It can't be found in the past or in the future, but in the nowness of lifeforms in the symbiotic real. It is the default way in which the past (trauma) sliding underneath the future (openness) generates a relative motion that doesn't have to be *chosen*, only *appreciated*.

When it becomes impossible to distinguish between behaving and acting, between executing an algorithm and being a person, we have entered a spectral realm. The notion of nonhumans as spectral is not cute or trivial. Indeed, spectrality could be thought as an index of reality or *accuracy*. How so? It has to do with the fact that ambiguity is a signal of accuracy.

When in the optician's the doctor hones in on your prescription, you face an inevitable choice between two different kinds of lens, either of which might work, but because they are so subtly different from one another it's hard to tell which one is better. The doctor asks, "Which one? Number one, or number two? Number one, or number two?" You might as well choose one or the other. The basic, irresolvable ambiguity that happens at that moment is a signal of the *accuracy* of the prescription. This is not how we normally like to think about ambiguity. We usually assume that ambiguity means that something is amiss. Here it means that given the physical constraints of the lenses and the constraints of your vision system, your ability to receive and interpret visual data, you are now seeing as well as you can. You won't ever see absolutely perfectly, because physical systems are necessarily determinate and therefore limited. The spectral realm is a space not of indeterminacy: zombies are very different from vampires; chickens are different from lemurs. It is a realm of profound ambiguity, with many more variables than the ones you find in the optometrist's chair.

The gap between the principle of (perfect) sight and the kind of sight you are achieving with the lenses becomes obvious, and so does something else. The gap between the two kinds of lens exists but you can hardly detect it. These two facts are deeply related. The lenses have been tuned to your vision. The space of attunement is a spectral realm that is "analog," thick, not rigidly bounded, so that more than one choice becomes available. The floating of decision in this spectral attunement space is *accurate*. And highly determinate.

Now consider just one thing, such as a tiny object close to absolute zero in a vacuum. This thing also begins to display determinate ambiguity, making us aware of a spectral attunement space. There are certain quantum phenomena, where a weird overlap between two physical systems—called superposition—can occur. The two lenses are different, yet in another way they are the same. Just as how the most accurate data perception format that we have (quantum theory and the equipment we build to observe quantum states) shows that when a thing is very carefully scrutinized, for instance at near absolute zero in a vacuum, it starts to reveal its profound ambiguity, exhibiting phenomena such as superposition or what is called coherence. Because of the finitude of a physical system, you can't hit absolute zero perfectly. But the system doesn't need to be absolutely at zero kelvin. What seems to be static and firm starts to reveal its shifty qualities: the way in which it is smeared into itself, or vibrating and not-vibrating at the same time, or shimmering without being pushed in a mechanical way.

The thing starts to show that it is *haunted*—by itself. Humankind is not a unified lump of blandness; it is a flickering hauntedness. Humankind does exist, but in the X-existence way. Solidarity thus X-exists in this way: it is always X-solidarity, inclusive of $1+n$ beings, not just one (human beings). *Solidarity implies nonhumans.*

Nonmeaning is haunted by meaning; meaning is a ghost that arrives yet never arrives. We can't find it at the end of the sentence—we can't find it at the end of all the sentences. Yet, sentences depend on it. Meaning is a specter that haunts signification. Justice, as Plato demonstrated, can never be directly seen, only embodied in imperfect instances of itself. Justice haunts the impossibility of perfect justice in any one instance. Forgiveness is haunted by the idea of forgiving the unforgiveable, which would be the ultimate kind of forgiveness—and also impossible. All kinds of biological and physical categories—life, mind, sentience, consciousness, even existence as such X-exist. Mind can't be reduced to matter, yet it can't be reduced to non-matter either.

Acting haunts behavior such that when we get very close to these concepts, we can't decide between them. Along with proving that bees can learn and teach other bees, that ants can hesitate, and that rats can experience regret, we can do something else, something cheaper in every sense. And more effective: endless proofs won't satisfy someone who thinks that there is no ambiguity between acting and behaving. What we can do is wonder whether, at this moment, I myself am a person or an android. Without bringing in a supreme being as a referee—it would have to be a benevolent one, too—it is impossible to tell. This is the true genius of Descartes' *Meditations*. Perhaps thinking that I imagine and act rather than simply execute algorithms is just the kind of thing that the android Tim Morton has been programmed to think.

Mind is neither inside nor outside the physical, inside nor outside my body. To exist is to be an uncanny doppelganger of oneself at the same time. Uncanny "inhuman" beings are not products of racism; they are the attempt to construct a "healthy human being" not haunted by its inhuman specter. It's right to accuse Nazi animal rights and Hitler's vegetarianism of being anthropocentric and indeed racist, based on an impossibly clean difference between the human and the nonhuman, enabled by exterminating the *unhuman* in social, psychic and philosophical space. Uncanny beings are not made uncanny. Being at all just is uncanny X-being. To feel solidarity is to feel haunted.

I DOUBT, THEREFORE I HAVE SOLIDARITY WITH YOU

Back to the optician's. Your final choice of lens two instead of lens one can't be perfect, if you think *perfect* means the one and only solution to your vision problem. Lens two will always be haunted by lens one. Lens two doesn't exhaust the possibility of attuning to your vision system. It is not perfectly *adequate* to your vision, like a key fitting a lock, which means that we are now in a truth domain that radically departs from the habit-forming medieval Neoplatonic monotheist concept of truth as adequation.[32]

It's also not the case that the lens is haunted by something like potentiality, another favorite way of domesticating the weirdness of actual physical things. According to this view, adopted by Agamben in a reading of Aristotle, potentiality is the openness in which all kinds of things could happen, while actuality is when this openness closes up.[33] But in the view I'm exploring here, there is a perfect overlap between potential and actual. What I'm saying here is that the *actual* lens is open, spectral, ambiguous, as a condition of possibility for its being a good-enough lens (and good-enough is as good as it gets). Spectrality, the way a thing keeps exceeding itself, or is displaced from itself, or is ecstatically outside itself (*ekstasis*, "ex-sistence"), doesn't just belong to human being, as Heidegger thought. Humankind is flickering, displaced from itself, ec-static, rippling and dappled with shadows. Shadows made not only by some other entity interacting with it, like the sun through the trees, but shadows that are an intrinsic part of the thing. When the lens is close enough to being "right," it starts to be haunted by the other lens, as if the other were so similar as to be uncannily the *same* lens. What stands outside the human is species-being as such, so that the ecstatic quality of Dasein is in fact non-anthropocentric, not to mention non-German and non-Nazi.

There is no need to distill the possibility of the possibility of the possibility of solidarity from some kind of void potential, in the way Agamben would proceed. The magical specter is right here.

Personal identity needs an upgrade to imagine the identity of species-being outside of a teleological metaphysics of presence and a toxic, overkill survival mode. Imagine an extremely accurate zombie or android version of yourself: the uncanny would consist in how impossible it would be to maintain that you were yourself anymore, exclusively and alone. "You" might as well be the android version! Your self-concept—I am me, here, and usually we emphasize this even more by thinking, I am a gas or liquid contained "in" this body here—evaporates. Uncanniness, paranoia and ambiguity are indices of reality, not of unreality.

One surprising conclusion we can draw now is that *paranoia is a possibility condition for empathy*. It's counterintuitive, but we can only conclude that empathy becomes distorted when it assumes that there is a definite person over there with definite shoes I can definitely walk in. What empathy requires is the energy of *solidarity*, vibrating away in the basement—I join with you even though I can't check in advance whether there is a *you* there. More and more and more detailed uncertainty as to the ontological status of a being looks and quacks like love. Empathy might involve a reification that is amplified in fully condescending sympathy, with its intrinsic power relationship. I am to decide whether or not to give you a coin as you beg on the street corner. Paranoia is co-emergent. It could go either way, toward reification when I try to reduce the paranoia, or toward solidarity when I don't.

This is problematic when it comes to sentient nonhumans, and more so when it comes to those nonhumans genetically closest to the human—not to mention the human as such. As one approaches the human, hardwired reductionism (cognitive, ethical, ontological) takes over: paranoia encourages us to reify. Theoretical physicists, with their heads in black holes and fermions, are the best defenders of the humanities for this reason, whereas neuroscientists, with their heads in our heads, do not have such a great track record:

> We can't ask a creature to [talk to] us, but we can observe behavior, ask sensible questions, create some good experiments, and come to a better understanding. Einstein did this with physics. Darwin with the tree of life. Galileo didn't complain . . . that the planets wouldn't talk to him . . . Yet because we cannot converse with other animals, animal behaviorists throw up their hands, saying we can't know if they think or feel, and we should assume they cannot.[34]

Confused by the rigid strong correlationism of the linguistic turn, many humanities scholars don't prevent this slide toward the most default support of the human–nonhuman boundary. The idea that the (human) subject or history or economic relations is the Decider and that the correlatee is a blank screen forecloses the paranoia. Think about emotion. We observe some emotions in nonhumans such as elephants, but we are less willing to let elephants feel emotions that seem less useful to us. We can let elephants be hungry when they look hungry, but we have trouble allowing that they are happy when they look happy.[35] That, for some reason, would be anthropomorphic and therefore bad. (What if worrying about anthropomorphism were itself a perfect example of human behavior, namely . . . anthropomorphism?)

It's interesting that we think sheer survival (hence hunger) is more "real" than a quality of existing, such as being happy. Just surviving, hunger, are supposedly "real" conditions, by which we mean nothing to do with being human in particular. Ecological catastrophe has been wrought in the name of this survival, sheer existence without heed to any quality of existence. This default utilitarianism has been very harmful to *us*, let alone to other life-forms. We think that what's good about it is that sheer survival is above and beyond our existence as humans! That bottom line statement says it all.

The division between "substantial" and "superficial" underwrites the difference between reality and appearance in the Twittersphere of truthiness, the spectral space in which truth and falsehood happen.[36] We believe sheer *behavior* to be on the side of reality—it's what we can observe empirically—whereas *action* is a mysterious aspect of how just one entity *behaves* (note the paradox). The metaphysical, onto-theological freight couldn't be easier to identify. Despite the lack of empirical verifiability, we are able to point to (human) action in the empirical realm, and we refrain abstemiously from anything like even wanting to point to action when it comes to nonhumans. But there is no reason for this division.

Normally, at this point in the argument, philosophy might reduce human acting to sheer behavior. This would reduce the paranoia, which wouldn't be good. But it's also very problematic, because if I'm just behaving when I reduce action like that, how can I check that what I'm doing is correct? I'm going to go the other way around. This doesn't mean granting nonhumans the ability to act. I'm interested in working away at that arbitrary division.

Utility is hugely overrated as a driver of lifeforms and of evolution. Sexual display is ridiculously expensive from DNA's point of view. Why even evolve it? It must be because of the way things are: reality isn't actually something bland "underneath" appearances, so that utility isn't something bland underneath more "pointless" goals. This distinction very much has to do with the profound ambiguity between acting and behaving. For Kant, a work of art behaves as if it is acting . . . rather like us. This ambiguity is a way to know that there is a gap between being and appearing that we can't point to—it's transcendental.

Kant argues that we know that there is a reality not because we can point to it or smack it or see it directly—that kind of validation can only be backed up by threats of violence, because it involves metaphysical beliefs—but because we are able to have a profoundly ambiguous, non-ego experience he calls beauty. Beauty is a spectral being that haunts me in my "inner" space, or rather, makes me aware that I am not "inside" something at all, but strangely blended with what I'm seeing "over there," so that I can't tell whose fault the beauty experience is, mine or the painting's.

Trying to locate the experience either "over here" or "over there" results in ruining it. If you think it's a certain feature of the *Mona Lisa,* say the smile, then a thousand photocopies of the smile should be a thousand times more beautiful than the actual experience you are having with it. But this can't be true. Or, if you think it's a certain feature of your response that you can locate, for example in your brain, for instance a certain neurotransmitter, then a thousand pills consisting of that neurotransmitter's active ingredient should in turn create an experience a thousand times more beautiful. But it won't. It will kill you.

Beauty is a strange experience because in it I get a feel for something I can't feel, or as Keats put it, "the feel of not to feel it."[37] I can't grasp the beauty experience without ruining it, so I need to leave it alone in its deep ambiguity, an ambiguity I often experience as a floating sadness without anything in particular to be sad about. "Sadness" here is happiness without a concept: "Sad is happy for deep people."[38] Sadness here does not have an object in particular: we aren't talking about melancholia, which is the trace of lost objects. Sadness is precisely without objectification, a spectral floating pleasure that cannot attach to an object because it is incapable of reification. It haunts me to the extent that it isn't cooked up by my ego, yet it is happening in my experiential space. It is part of me, yet it isn't. Sadness is beauty in all its spectral strangeness.

BEAUTY IS HAUNTED

How come I can have an experience that is beyond my ego? Because I'm not completely me! I'm full of holes because I am like everything else, a living, breathing malfunction made up of all kinds of things that aren't me, that misbehave constantly. Such an experience beyond ego is an incontrovertible refutation of solipsism without need for further empirical validation, because even if the universe is only me, there are two of me. Or there is just me and my hallucination, a being that isn't me. Moreover, the other me pesters me all the time, so I don't get a moment's peace. I am shimmering. Furthermore, I can't decide whether this really is me, or the effect of some other being. Beauty means being haunted by another entity, which might or might not be me, but this is radically undecidable.

At a more fundamental level yet, and a more bizarre one, the spectrality of a table that can move by itself without mechanical input—and its implication in the world of the paranormal—is precisely at issue. Metaphors can get away from their creators; like dancing tables they can misbehave and slip out a truth that the author didn't intend. If Marx is saying that a dancing table is necessarily absurd, such that a computing table (one that evolves notions out of its wooden brain) is even more absurd, then Marx is cleaving implicitly to a substance ontology in which appearing is separated from being, and in which subject is separated from object, and in which there is a logic that allows for no contradictions and no excluded middles. This is unfortunate because Marx himself argues that capitalism promulgates a substance ontology, borrowing an argument from Aristotle. Aristotle says of the concept of matter that it's like searching through a zoo to find the "animal" rather than the various species such as monkeys and mynah birds.[39] What Aristotle says about matter, Marx says about capital.

Things can't move by themselves because this would violate the Law of Noncontradiction. The mover of the table must be moved mechanically, not by itself or telekinetically. The spectacle of its movement must be a false appearance. But this would be to accept the *non-strangeness* of the computing table that evolves notions out of its wooden brain. The table can appear to think. The thinking table confronts us with the paranoia of artificial intelligence: we can never prove if it's a person or not.

But if the dancing table isn't really dancing, it means that the table isn't really thinking. This would mean that commodity fetishism doesn't function at all—but this can't be correct! The reduction of strangeness abolishes the idea of commodity fetishism. Marx here appears to have a foot in the world of solidarity with nonhumans. The friendly comedy with which he talks about such things as tables and coats might also indicate this. Marx *almost accepts* tables that dance by themselves or that are moved by telekinesis.

Since the ambiguity between acting and behaving is part of a larger ambiguity between being alive and not being alive, to embrace the specter of the nonhuman fully is to embrace the specter of *anything at all* being "alive" in the sense of moving without mechanical input. If this is true, it eats away at the biocentric and biopolitical notion of Life as opposed to non-life. Furthermore, to embrace these specters is to embrace spectrality, which is to say, the way in which appearing and being are impossible to separate in such a way that a basic ontological ambiguity is a possibility condition for existence as such.

What is ideological is that the dancing table is strapped down and forced to compute (human) values. Assuming that the table is an unformatted surface, that it's only what it is when (human) economic relations format it—either because it's unformed matter or because it's a blank screen for human desire—is part and parcel of reification, and the reason why capitalism works. If communism is going to transcend capitalism, it has to transcend this anthropocentric, "overmining" mode; otherwise it becomes only a variant of the logistics that gave rise to capitalism in the first place.

Marxism *doesn't work* and therefore *will not survive* without including nonhuman beings in its construction. Moreover, including nonhuman beings implies also including spectrality. And this means tables can dance. And this means the distinction between "lifeform" and "table" breaks down in some sense.

PERFORATED WORLDS

Let's return to the concept of *world*. World is a profoundly Heideggerian concept—it has to do with how Dasein co-creates or correlates or Decides on reality (whichever term you prefer). For Heidegger, humans are the ones with a full world: world is a process, *worlding*, and humans are the *worlding* beings. And German humans are the best at worlding.

Heidegger's Nazism is more than unfortunate, and it's a shame that the reaction to him is so often blanket condemnation, while at the same time using his terminology, or generating concepts within his thought region, concepts that have "–ality" and "–icity" suffixes.

But the good news is that like Marx's anthropocentrism, Heidegger's Nazism is a bug, not a feature. The metaphysics of presence that allows one to point to Germans as the best world-ers is in fact illegal within Heidegger's thought. Furthermore, the notion of world only works if we allow nonhumans to have it. Heidegger says that "animals" are "poor in world" (*Weltarm*) and inanimate beings such as stones have no world at all. But in truth, not only can we allow cats to have a world, but even waterfalls. We can do this because *world* is very cheap. We don't have to raise cats and waterfalls up to human status to do so, and this is great for another reason. If world is a prize for being special, the trajectory within the concept is inevitably toward Nazism. But if instead world is an incredibly cheap thing that worms can have, it's not that worms can be Nazis, but that Nazis are just very confused, puffed-up worms.

Why is world cheap? Because world is inherently lacking, inherently ragged and faulty. World is *perforated*. There are not perfect, smoothly functioning worlds, and poor people's versions. To have a world intrinsically is to be *Weltarm*.[40] World is *only* ever something you can be poor in, not because you didn't get to enjoy it as much as an SS officer, but because world as such is poverty. *World* is structurally, irreducibly perforated:

> I read the news today, oh boy
> Four thousand holes in Blackburn, Lancashire
> And though the holes were rather small
> They had to count them all
> Now they know how many holes it takes to fill the Albert Hall.
> (The Beatles, "A Day in the Life")[41]

This is also marvelous in another way: if there is no such thing as a full world, there is no such thing as no world at all. So even water-falls have worlds! World is cheap enough for everything to have it. In this reality, there is not (full) world or no world at all; there is a range of overlapping worlds.

This cheapness saves us from the popular cul-de-sac of *world* as a normative concept. We sometimes hear that worlding is a special property of lifeforms, and held up as a reason to care for those lifeforms. To some extent, it is. World doesn't depend on conscious-ness. It's not about *knowing* that there is a world. It's about getting on with stuff, going about your doggy, or spidery, or whaley busi-ness. But "saving the world" doesn't mean preserving a world. There is a world of precarious, cheap labor, of massively underpaid, overexploited workers in electronics factories in China. Does that mean that these factories should be protected or cared for?

The cheapness of world also saves us from the blanket condem-nation of world.[42] Of course world doesn't make sense as a meta-physically present entity you can point to; it never did. But that doesn't mean it doesn't exist at all. It just means that your idea of "exist" needs an upgrade, an upgrade that deconstruction (Heidegger, Derrida) makes readily available. *The end of the world* is the end of a normative, white Western world that takes itself to be coherent and smooth and top.

Heidegger argues that what he calls worldview is bad because it is reified and solid. But his opposing concept of world is also solid, and it malfunctions in his thought because of this fake perfection. Because of ecological awareness, you are experiencing your world as malfunctioning, as broken, precisely insofar as all kinds of things are sticking out of the normalized background we take to be our world, which most often is deeply anthropocentrically scaled. All kinds of unexpected things are emerging from melting Arctic ice: methane, Cold War bases . . . things trapped deep, and thoughts and assumptions trapped deep in our unconscious minds, too.

But through this malfunctioning one comes to realize some-thing deep. The notion of (smooth, complete) world as such is also broken. There is no way to put it back together, because the very concept of smooth functioning, just happening without things sticking out, is anthropocentrically scaled. Worlds are not like that. This means that we have transformed our idea of world. World precisely *is* this tattered, perforated patchwork quilt that doesn't quite start and stop with a definite horizon—temporal as well as spatial horizons are equally full of holes and blurry, by the way.

In turn this means we can *share* worlds. Our human world is shared with all kinds of other tattered, broken worlds. The world of spiders, the world of tigers, the world of bacteria. Wittgenstein was wrong: we *can* understand lions—at least to some extent. This isn't because we condescendingly expand our world, but because our world is perforated—we don't quite understand *ourselves*, either. We can understand tigers and ourselves modally: we can share worlds 20 percent, or 60 percent. Sharing doesn't have to be all or nothing. World sharing requires regular violations of the Law of the Excluded Middle.

We just upgraded, or rather downgraded, world to a manifold that is intrinsically inviting to nonhuman beings. This is better than giving up on world altogether, and asserting that there is no world at all—that is also anthropocentric. It's like saying that since I can't play with this soccer ball, no one else is allowed to play with it either. Perforated worlds can overlap. This cat isn't a guest in my house; it's a member of the family, which isn't really *my* family, and I can think this not by elevating the cat into some special condescendingly bestowed status, but by noticing that my perforated world intersects with his. By noticing that family is also a symbiotic relationship that is uneasy and contingent, not a solid world with a smooth boundary. We are both guests of each other, guests of the house, and the house is a guest of ourselves.

The world concept is in the form of a form of verb, worlding, because it's best thought as the emergent property of an algorithmic process. You get on with things, and your world emerges from this getting on. You cook, go to the shops, kiss your boyfriend, start a reading group, break your toe and hobble to the hospital, quit your job, go on a march. That's your world. We have a tendency to think that world is solid and rigid and perfect because of the algorithm of agrilogistics functioning in the background of social space.

World is always spectral. World is the noise your behavior makes. World has a virtual, modal quality about it that you can't delete. Worlds are partial objects, like everything else. They are more than the wholes of which they are parts. There are many, many worlds in the biosphere, and these worlds are not just components of the biosphere, in the same way that the family isn't *my* family in particular.

Worlds are functions of algorithms, and algorithms can be more or less detailed and include many or few instructions and involve more or fewer beings. This means that the logic that describes worlds must be modal, a matter of *more* and *less* rather than *existing* or *not-existing*. A very complex recipe for an intricate dessert might create a rather elaborate world, whereas a stone resting at the bottom of a pond might not. A Palestinian hurling a stone at a police officer might be part of a very complex world indeed, emerging from an algorithm containing a lot of steps and confusing lines of code. But Palestinians and stones and dessert chefs can all share their worlds, or not, because their worlds are intrinsically perforated. We can talk to a lion, and we can listen to a lion. Cats have figured out how to talk with humans—in our company they develop a whole range of miaows. And isn't this evidence of how language as such isn't an exclusively human thing, and that human language itself can contain nonhuman terms? Cats don't magically learn to speak human. It's that humans use nonhuman words, because language is much less exclusive and special than we like to think—because worlds are intrinsically perforated. *Miaow*, like a car indicator light or an address on an envelope, has meaning and relevance because it's part of a set of interacting projects. *Miaow* relates to breasts and milk. Human babies are just like cats: they learn to vocalize a sound that connects the mother's breast to their lips.

Consciousness, language, world: it's not that there's no such thing as these entities. It's that they are so much cheaper than we reckoned they were. Nagel and Wittgenstein claim we can't identify at all with the worlds of bats and lions. But can we identify with *human worlds*?[43] Can we even identify with *our own worlds*? What does *identify* mean, if identity isn't all it's cracked up to be in the first place? Of course we can share the world of a lion, and she or he can share ours.

MODAL BEINGS

Georg Cantor showed that there is a gap between numbers and sets of numbers. Likewise, there is a gap between lifeforms and sets of lifeforms. We can think of these sets as ecosystems, biomes, biospheres—we can think of these sets at any scale, and there is no easy continuity between these sets. An environment just is a certain set of lifeforms. The way one does ecological research is to establish a somewhat arbitrary set: to define a boundary sometimes called a mesocosm, in which one observes lifeforms coming and going, reproducing, struggling.

An ecosystem is vague, in the sense that sorites paradoxes arise when one attempts to define them precisely. How many blades of grass do I have to remove for this meadow not to be a meadow? One—surely not. Two—still a meadow. Three, four, and so on— and the same logic applies until I have only one blade of grass left. I conclude, wrongly, that there is no meadow. These paradoxes plague sets of lifeforms at any scale, and therefore it's strictly impossible to think ecological reality via a metaphysics of presence, namely, a belief that to be a thing, you have to be constantly present.

Sorites paradoxes exist everywhere in ecological thought, because ecological beings are heaps: ecosystems, boundaries between geological eras, lifeforms . . . We'll see how necessary it is to believe they exist as we proceed. To believe in them, we need a logic that allows them to exist.

It's much better to think that there is a meadow and there is not a meadow at the same time. We will violate the supposed Law of Noncontradiction, but it wasn't that great for lifeforms anyway. There is a meadow, but we can't point to it directly, because it's not constantly present. And yet here is the meadow, with the butterflies, the cowslips, the voles. Just as a vole is a set of things that are not voles, so the meadow is a set of things such as voles that are not meadows. A meadow is an implosive whole made of partial objects.

Thus, a spectral strangeness that haunts being applies not only to lifeforms—a vole is a not-vole—but also to meadows, ecosystems, biomes and the biosphere. The haunting, ungraspable yet vivid spectrality of things also means that there can be sets of things that are not strictly members of those sets, violating Russell's prohibition on the set paradox that arises through thinking Cantor's transfinite sets. Transfinite sets are sets of numbers that contain sets of numbers that are not strictly members of that set. There is an irreducible gap between the set of real numbers and the set of rational numbers—Cantor and Gödel drove themselves crazy trying to find a smooth continuum between the two.

The idea that there is a soul or even a mind that is "in" a body like a gas in a bottle is an attempt to contain and reduce the spectrality. But this reification is a mistake. The mistake people are making here is to onticize spectrality, to make the specter something you can point to "here" and "at this time," whereas the specter is an *ontological* aspect of the structure of how things are. The spectrality of a thing is more like a medical syndrome, a chronic symptom that's hard to detect, and less like a point on a map. An object and its uncanny spectral halo form an *objectitis*. We can generate another meaning for the word "dance" in *Capital*: a dancing table is simply a regular old table, but one to which we have restored the spectrality so that there is a dance between the table and its spectral halo, like "ghosting" on VHS tape.

So many specters, so little time. Anarchism is the specter of Marxism and some of its spectrality must be let back in to allow Marxism to breathe in an environment in which it accommodates nonhumans. And consumerism is the specter of environmental-ism, such that the future enhancement and multiplication of pleasure modes implied in ecological awareness and ecological social policy draws on and amplifies phenomenological chemicals manufactured in the heart of the enemy of vanilla environmentalisms.

To repeat: Marxism *doesn't work* and therefore *will not survive* without including nonhuman beings. And including nonhuman beings implies also including spectrality. And this means tables can dance. And this means the distinction between "lifeform" and "table" breaks down in some sense. Marxism only works if it weirdly embraces animism. Is saying this appropriating First Peoples' culture? I understand the concern, but as I pointed out in the introduction, the philosophical source of this anxiety is a strong correlationism that underwrites imperialism, especially in its early phase. The British were only too happy to draw sharp lines of cultural difference between themselves and the subjugated people whose habits "just aren't cricket."

THE SPACE OF SPECTRAL POLITICS

Biopolitics involves the demarcation, classification and control of beings according to concepts of life. It has created a control society whose zero-level structure is that of the death camp. What comes after biopolitics? The politics of undeath. It must, because relying on what comes *before* biopolitics has to do with subjects and objects, which has to do with souls and bodies, which is precisely a resistance to the spectral. Subjects and objects depend on proprietary notions of selfhood, in which I am I because I am in possession of myself.

We could joke that including nonhumans in this setup is both difficult and impossible. Difficult, because extending the self-concept to include nonhumans is highly onerous and fraught with paradoxes. Prove that *I myself as a human* have a self-concept. Waiting for a human to allow a chimp to have a self-concept so that the chimp can be liberated from what is now taken to be its prison (a zoo) might well mean that the chimp dies before a verdict can be reached.[44] Impossible, because if everything has rights, then nothing has rights, because rights depend on possessing things, and if nothing can be a possession, then nothing can have rights.

What comes next is not an expansion of rights, but an attunement of solidarity, to varying degrees of sharpness and amplitude. Spectral space is highly differentiated. It is nothing to do with life as survival. Yet it is not in the service of a one-size-fits-all life-as-abundance. It isn't so easy to tell between a ghost and a person, between a person and an algorithm, between intelligence and computation, between number and counting. They each entail the other. And yet there is a very sharp difference at the same time. Much Western philosophy tries to contain the ghostly oscillation between these categories by policing the difference or by making it ontic—something you can point to. This is how racism and speciesism work. Racism says that the essence of the human can be pointed out in ontic space-time. Speciesism says the same in a different key. This pointing can't happen. But a human is not a rabbit.

In the previous chapter, I pointed out that capitalism is a machine for producing in social space the object as imagined by default Western ontology: a bland lump of extension decorated with accidents. Alienating my specific, sensuous labor, homogenous abstract labor time is like a soul that capitalism forces into my body, making me into a Cartesian or Aristotelian zombie, a tool with a soul. In a way, capitalism strips the spectrality from things and forces properly behaved souls down their throats instead. This full-bodied yet totally bland abstraction is what is left of creativity and creations. How I'm molding this chocolate doesn't exhaust me, or the chocolate, or the mold: there are other possibilities. Withdrawal—the fact that no access mode can exhaust a thing— bestows upon things their flickering, spectral quality. Capitalism tries to eliminate withdrawal, as if it could be wiped away; the fact that nothing can eliminate this ontological feature is why capitalism is violent.

Communism is spectral insofar as enjoyment and creation modes don't need to be exhausted by the social format of economic system requirements. In particular, my production doesn't have to be "for me," but can be aimed toward a future in which I don't exist, or a part of the biosphere where I don't exist, or exist less. Production can be "useless," insofar as it doesn't serve my ego or the ego of a particular economic mode. All the different ways I can handle chocolate, and the ways chocolate can handle me, and the ways other beings can handle chocolate, are irrelevant to *this* specific state of how capital extracts *this* specific value at *this* specific historical moment. In a while, the hoover will move on to extract value differently. It doesn't even care about the specifics of how it's hoovering right now.

Humankind is a thing, and so it withholds its graspability, it is open. Humankind is humankind, not some abstract being but a very specific one. Yet this doesn't mean we can point to it directly. Humankind is *specific* and *spectral*. The quality of humankindness floats spectrally like a halo around humans, precisely because of the specificity. The logic here is subtractive. We can say *less* about beings than we thought, and this is what makes them sensual, not some fullness of presence. They aren't fully present, so there is less of them around to point to. Capitalism tries to bring them to full presence in the commodity format, but this presence isn't luscious, it's bland and merely extensional. Lusciousness is found in *less than presence*.

If humankind is less than Life, and less than being a special life-form, and less even than being a lifeform at all, then we need to explain something. What is this "less than"?

3

Subscendence

It is believed that one cannot be more than man. Rather, one cannot be less!

—Max Stirner, *The Ego and Its Own*

Idris: Are all people like this?
The Doctor: Like what?
Idris: So much bigger on the inside.

—*Doctor Who*

"The whole is greater than the sum of its parts." This truism is one of the most profound inhibitors of world sharing. This kind of holism is a symptom of agricultural-age monotheism that we are still retweeting, even if we think we are atheists. Its belief format is evident in the way in which Gestalt psychology is misheard to be repeating it. Gestalt psychology argues that the whole is *different* than its parts, not *greater than*, yet this common misunderstanding persists among psychologists.[1] We must find some tools to dismantle it. Why not rewrite holism such that the whole is always *less* than the sum of its parts? Let's call it "subscendence." We'll go about proving this by examining some features of object-oriented ontology.

We should see things such as humankind as wholes that are less than the sum of their parts. Tim Morton is so many more things than just "human." A street full of people is much more than just a part of a greater whole called "city." It's hard to locate contemporary megacities because we keep looking for something that totally incorporates its parts. Towns, villages and other formations are strung together in Java in such a way that only the volcanoes on that massive island prevent them from spreading everywhere. The only limit is a perceived threat to life. The string of dwellings isn't even a megacity, it's a *hypercity*, a city that is hardly a city at all. But precisely because of this less-than-a-city quality, a hypercity is beyond even the colossal size we associate with megacities such as Mexico City. Java's hypercity and Mexico City are less than the sum of their parts. Parts of them—houses, regions of houses— keep on pouring out of them like ice cubes bursting through the paper bag they made wet.

Wholes *subscend* their parts, which means that parts are not just mechanical components of wholes, and that there can be genuine surprise and novelty in the world, that a different future is always possible. It is good to regard things such as capitalism as physical beings, not simply as fictions that would disappear if we just stopped believing in them. But what kind of physical being are they? If they are subscendent, it means that we can change them, if we want. What if some things could be physically huge, yet ontologically tiny? What if neoliberalism, which envelopes Earth in misery, were actually quite small in another way, and thus strangely *easy* to subvert? Too easy for intellectuals, who want to make everything seem difficult so they can keep themselves in a job by explaining it, or outdo each other in competition for whose picture of the world is more depressing. "I am more intelligent than you because my picture of neoliberalism is far more terrifying and encompassing than yours. We are *truly* enslaved in my vision, with no hope of escape—therefore I am superior to you!" Isn't this a tragic consequence of what some call *cynical reason*, the dominant way of being right for the last two hundred years?

To prove subscendence is also childishly simple, which makes the resistance you will feel toward it all the more significant. To show that the whole is less than the sum of its parts, all you need to do is accept that a group of things can be a thing, which is a simple way of saying that if a thing exists, it exists *in the same way* as another thing. A sentence exists in the same way as a word processing program. A tree exists in the same way as a forest. An idea exists in the same way as a quasar. This is very far from saying that things have the same *right* to exist. Claiming that the AIDS virus has as much right to exist as an AIDS patient is a conclusion you can draw within the logic of deep ecology, but it has nothing to do with actual ecological politics, and everything to do with a Gaia hypothesis or concept of a biosphere that is greater than the sum of its parts, in which every being is a replaceable component. This has to do with agricultural-age religion, the ideological support of the social, psychic and philosophical machination that eventually generated mass extinction. Deep ecology is fighting fire with fire.

Very well, a tree exists in the same way as a forest. The forest is ontologically one. The trees are more than one. The parts of the forest (the trees—but there are so many more parts in fact) outnumber the whole. This doesn't mean they "are more important than the whole." This is the kind of anti-holist reductionism that neoliberalism promotes: "There is no such thing as society; there are only individuals." We need holism, but a special, weak holism that isn't theistic.

Climate is ontologically smaller than weather. Weather is a symptom of climate, but there is so much more to weather other than simply being a symptom of climate. A shower of rain is a bath for this bird. It's a spawning pond for these toads. It's this soft delicate pattering on my arm. It's this thing I wrote some sentences about.

Humankind is ontologically smaller than the humans who make it up! There is so much more that humans do other than be parts of humankind. Humans modify their bodies to change their gender and add electronic and decorative prostheses. Humans form relationships with nonhumans. Humans contain nonhumans such as the bacterial microbiome in such a way that if the nonhumans left, the humans would die.

This means that the correct left concept of the human is of a *partial object* in a set of partial objects, such that it comprises an *implosive whole* that is less than the sum of its parts. This partiality extends in every dimension, including time. An event is a temporal partial object. An event is part of some set of events that comprises a whole, but this whole is always less than the sum of its parts. A battle in feudal Japan was not simply a matter of two lords fighting. Flies settled on the corpses. Five years later, delicate flowers bloomed. Evolution shuffled the decks in its eons-long game of cards.

To be a thing is to be a perforated bag full of water, in which are swimming countless little perforated bags full of water, in which are floating . . . When you cut open a bag, so many more bags spill out than you probably bargained for. This is how an emotional label such as "anger" is *not* (quite evidently) a whole that intuitively contains gradations and subtleties all comprehensively summed up by that one term. We may find within it hesitation, a sense of humor, sexual passion, grief. This is equivalent to discovering that a physical line has a fractal dimensionality when you examine it more closely. A fractal is a *partial number* that goes wiggling around being just itself for a potential infinity of iterations. Beauty is slightly disgusting or weird or fascinating because the human-scaled bag full of water that is inducing the beauty experience inevitably contains and is part of bags full of water at all kinds of nonhuman scales. Kitsch is subscendent beauty. What Bataille calls "general economy" is a subscendent twelve-inch remix of restricted economy. And what this means is that all the nonhuman economic modes are in the mix too. Economics is really just about how you organize enjoyment. And ecological politics just means allowing and enhancing all kinds of enjoyment that aren't obviously to do with you. Well, not that they're nothing to do with you—that's too tight. It's just that you let yourself be perforated.

Spectrality means that a being is a symbiotic community consisting of itself and its spectral halo. A being is less than the sum of its parts. Kitsch is other people's enjoyment. In an ecological age, where there is no one true and proper scale, beauty will be appreciated along with its halo of weirdness or disgust. This kind of beauty is X-beauty, just like a lifeform is always an X-lifeform. Marxism that includes nonhumans is a subscendent X-Marxism, less than the sum of Marxism and anarchism (and so on). Political space that includes nonhumans is X-space that subscends its parts.

OF INVISIBLE GODS

Not everything can be empirically observed. There are some things that are thinkable and computable, yet we find it impossible to see them: the hyperobjects. Many are ecological phenomena such as global warming, evolution and extinction, not to mention the human species and the biosphere.

We tend to think of these things as wholes that are greater than the sum of their parts, but let's see how they subscend their parts. The political task we face is to see physically gigantic and intellectually complex (hence invisible) things as ontologically tiny. Neoliberalism is physically vast, but ontologically small. We are able to dismantle it, by crawling out from underneath in solidarity with the other lifeforms it now threatens.

But if "the whole is greater than the sum of its parts" is true, it doesn't really matter if those parts get replaced. We will still have our lovable old whole intact. Say the whole is the biosphere and say the part, which we very much imagine as a component because of the holism, is a polar bear. Never mind. They will go extinct and another lifeform will simply have to evolve to take their place. This kind of thought might not be so good for ecological ethics and politics.

Adherents of OOO hold that an entity contains a potentially infinite regress of other entities. The entity is literally out-scaled by its parts. It is bigger on the inside, like Pandora's jar. Which means, logically, that it's smaller on the outside, so that, however absurd and amazing it sounds, we need to say "the whole is always smaller than the sum of its parts." The fact that hyperobjects subscend their parts is why you can't find them. Global warming and the biosphere are ontologically small, which means that they are fragile since they can be overwhelmed by their very components—even black holes evaporate after emitting too much Hawking radiation, and nothing at all other than themselves can destroy *them*. Married couples in the United States are taxed as one-and-a-half people. Ontologically, a married couple is smaller than two unmarried people. Married couples are famously fragile.

Notice that the subscendence of the whole from the parts doesn't contradict the fact that there is an intrinsic excess in a thing whereby it's never exhausted by its appearances. Conversely, a thing is withdrawn *not* because it is a lump of dough *hiding behind* appearances, but because it *subscends* its appearances in a way that is not constantly present. There can be more appearances than things. Since causality happens in the realm of appearance, this gives us the reason why novelty can happen, and novelty is the crucial ingredient of revolution. The fact that we have trouble understanding these paradoxes is a symptom of how we have become habituated to going in the direction of *transcendence* toward a *more constant presence*.

All this means that what things are subscends how they appear, which is how appearance comes to be death. Even a hypothetical lonesome object all on its very own, such as a black hole, will end precisely because its essence subscends its appearance. A thing subscends its appearances. Isn't that the definition of dying? I become memories in you, pieces of crumpled paper in a wastebasket, a corpse, some loose change. These appearances exceed me and I'm distributed into a weird, intangible intimacy. Appearance never expresses the whole, or let alone anything greater than the whole. Hyperobjects disappear "downwards," not upwards, into something paradoxically *more* physical and thus more fragile than the beings that comprise them. This explains for instance the viscosity of hyperobjects, the fact that they stick to you phenomenologically wherever you are. Their hyperphysicality is what makes them so sticky, closer than breathing, nearer than hands and feet: the mercury in my cells, the radiation streaming through my DNA. The subscendence we discover in hyperobjects suggests we might already have passed across a limit confining thought (even atheist thought) to Axial Age religious dogma. An end to the idea of huge, overarching, tyrannical beings that are bigger than us tiny, insignificant flies they use for their sport.

Subscendence is not the same as individualism. Individualism means that individuals are *more real* than groups or wholes. Individualism in the political sphere is well expressed by neoliberal politicians: "There is no such thing as society" (Margaret Thatcher). According to subscendence, wholes and parts are just as real as one another. It is simply that the whole is less than the sum of its parts. We could build a logic square, in fact, to make this clear:

(1) Whole is more real than parts

(2) Whole is greater than parts

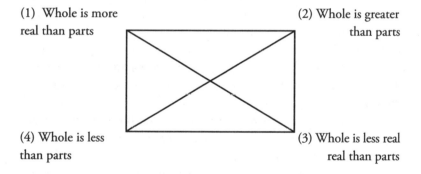

(4) Whole is less than parts

(3) Whole is less real than parts

Figure 2. Explosive and Implosive Holism

"Greater than" must mean "having more qualities than." "More real than" must mean "having more essence than." The "magic of the marketplace" and the systems-theory fascination with emergence are definitely at position (2): the whole and the parts are as real as one another, but in such a way that the whole has more qualities than the sum of its parts. Yet the neoliberalism that proclaims this is at position (3): the whole is greater—but less real! This explains how (2) can be deployed as a disguised form of individualism. But now we can see how this individualism is based on a stunning paradox.

We are fascinated with it even if we are not free market ideologues. It provides a way of having one's individualist cake and eating it—subsuming it into the whole—at the same time. In addition, emergentism requires that the parts are less real (position 1). The parts in this sense are just replaceable components, when one strips away the charming foliage of Gaia theory.

The way (1) can slip into (2) alerts us to the religious origins of standard holism, which is based on the default agrilogistic ontology. According to this ontology, "having more qualities than" cannot be distinguished from "having more essence than" because to exist must mean to totally and definitely exist, as opposed to not exist. If something is more vivid than something else, it must be more existent. There is no room for quasi-existing, shadowy, spectral existing shot through with nothingness. "More real than" and "greater than" become impossible to distinguish.

In the case of subscendence, it is not the case that the whole is less real or more real. "Less than" becomes possible to distinguish from "less real than." Wholes cannot be machines in the sense that they are made of replaceable components. It's simply religious mystification to claim that the biosphere or the state transcends little me in the sense that I become a replaceable component of a larger machine. Likewise, the Enlightenment inversion, namely that the parts (the individuals) are more real than the whole, is also the same mystification, just upside-down. In this sense, Marx was exactly right to view Enlightenment philosophy as a form of mystification. But he was wrong to think of Enlightenment (capitalist) economic theory as *fetishism*, as indigenous belief living on in a disillusioned age—*made out of disillusion*, in fact, in a cynical twist of history. The theory of fetishism is different from First Peoples' cultures but identical to Axial Age religion, though in inverted form. Indeed, this is the view that is most like the idea that inanimate things are possessed with a soul. Yahweh breathes life into clay. The *res intellectus* sits inside the extensional body, in Descartes. The soul drives the chariot of the body, in Plato. The Jesuits used the Tibetan word for "zombie" to describe the resurrected Christ and the Tibetans were understandably revolted.

If wholes are always smaller than their parts, neoliberalism is smaller than cynical reason has cracked it up to be. It isn't an angry god trying to kill me, but something that is *too easy* (for performances of intellectual sophistication) to subvert, for instance by unplugging a small German town from the oil-based energy grid.[2] What is required is a critical "gnosticism"—not the cartoon pathologized version that separates soul and body, but the heretical one, in which believing in a vast, angry Neolithic god that is so high you can't get around him, is precisely the problem. Bakunin: "These divine particles, human souls, retain as it were a vague remembrance of their primitive divinity, and are irresistibly drawn towards their whole; they seek each other, they seek their whole."[3]

The fragility of hyperobjects is political good news. Cynical reason has been lamenting neoliberalism as the inescapable psychopath Cthulhu—it loves this kind of doom-speak. But ontologically, neoliberalism is quite small compared to a polar bear. Maybe this kind of thinking is what distinguishes an anarchist from a Marxist, or at any rate a certain kind of successful academic Marxist. That kind of ideology theorist is really just a believer in Ra, someone mindlessly retweeting an agrilogistic meme that has been wildly successful in transforming Earth into a narrow temporality-diameter extinction pipe.

Subscendence affects things like nation-states, as huge and powerful as they appear. Subscendence is why you need a passport. It's not to guarantee your identity, but to guarantee and prop up the identity of the state. Islamophobia sees Muslim terrorists as inevitably part of some larger, shadowy organization, while in the United States, white terrorists are always described as "lone wolves." No matter how many of them shoot people in churches and outside abortion clinics and blow up government buildings, having trained in the Christian equivalent of an al-Qaeda training camp; no matter how many wolves there are, they are always seen as lone wolves, not as members of a pack.[4] The concept that wholes are greater than the sum of their parts comes in ideologically handy because then Islamophobia can claim that Islamic terrorists are part of some emergent, shadowy whole, while white terrorists are individuals without a whole in sight.

HUMANKIND IS A SUBSCENDENT WHOLE

Subscendent wholes are fuzzy and ragged. They involve an uncountable number of parts. The effect of this is to cause the whole to be weirdly shrunken.

Contextual criticism in the humanities has become sclerotic. Rather than the dangerous frisson of noticing a historical unconscious, what has become routine is to explain a cultural document away by "situating" it in a context that usually takes the shape of a decade within a particular century and pertains to the country and the specific region in which the document was produced. Needless to say, all these contextual features are thought in an anthropocentric way. We are talking about what it was like for humans when the painting was made, not what it was like for mice. But contextualization is potentially highly explosive: a cultural document subscends its contexts. There is no good reason to stop. Ironically most contextual criticism is trying to *contain* what is most interesting about context. And we can test this by thinking about ecology.

The thing about ecological contexts is that you can't draw a line around them in advance, because ecology is profoundly about interdependence. The biosphere depends on Earth's magnetic shield to protect lifeforms from solar rays, and this depends on the way Earth's iron core is spinning, and that depends on how the Earth formed in the early stages of the Solar System, and so on. We are dealing with a potential infinity of entities on a potential infinity of scales—there is no way to ascertain whether the pleroma of beings has an end point, at least not in advance. Ecological aware-ness just is this context explosion.

Very large entities such as mountains and oceans sometimes move in such a way that the vibrations of their movement create sound, far too deep for humans to hear. The sound waves travel across Earth, sweeping up all kinds of entities in their waveforms. You can record and broadcast this infrasound, but you have to build a special, very long speaker to push the wave through effi-ciently, and you have to speed it up about eighty times, so that humans can hear it—an incredibly deep, loud roar. It's like the soft roar that is part of the signature of an explosion: not the shattering, but the pervasive rumble.

Infrasound is literally the sound of context, exploding. And the way it explodes undermines the idea of nicely bounded wholes that poof out big enough to contain their parts in a nice unified group. The longer the description of all the elements of such a thing goes on, the more it threatens to open up an abyss. Wholes might be boreholes that go so deep down that we can't fathom their depth.

Infrasound is a Tolstoy novel about mountains, oceans and deserts. It is a perfect example of our current Age of Asymmetry: an ecological age in which we have so much more scientific data about things, which makes the things appear so much huger and more mysterious so that increasing knowledge doesn't master objects. There is, instead, a Cold War–like explosion of knowledge and withdrawnness at the same time, and for the same reason. This is a sharp difference from Hegel's picture of art history, in which knowledge gradually outstrips art materials, resulting, from the late eighteenth century on, in irony and the art of successful fail-ures to embody spirit.[5] That picture is just a symptom of the hubris that marks the beginning of the Anthropocene, which we have been calling modernity. But the impetus to transcend one's mate-rial conditions in every respect has resulted in drilling down, liter-ally, ever deeper into them, to the extent that now we have realized that this very movement has created far larger and more immersive material conditions than ever before. Global warming lasts for a hundred thousand years. This Age of Asymmetry turns out not even to be neatly asymmetrical. It's not really about humans full of inner space versus nonhumans also full of inner space. Because it's at this very moment that humans discover that they are one of those objects, precisely insofar as we are now allowing them all to be Pandora's jars like us, to contain multitudes.

Subscendence guarantees that objects encounter us as if they were the flu, getting inside our own fuzzy, ragged boundaries and executing their operations from an intimate place. Subscendence means, therefore, that we humans really aren't nihilistic negation monsters, but chameleon-like entities that are susceptible to colors, surfaces, sound waves—the way the flesh at the back of my eye is palpated by electromagnetic waves spraying out of an excited yttrium-oxide coating on the inside of an LCD display or cathode ray tube. I see red because yttrium waves are splashing onto me. Because I'm not a rigidly bounded whole but a ragged, subscendent one, I can wave along with this redness for a moment.

Susceptibility is very good news for ecological ethics and politics. I can be touched. Thinking itself is touching and being touched, not a guarantee of full metaphysical presence, but a disorienting flicker that haunts me or pleasures me or hurts me, and so on. A visual artist knows that visuality is badly misrepresented by philosophies that use the language of sight to establish constantly present things-to-be-seen, and the too-easy linkage of seeing and knowing. Perhaps ecological philosophy needs to generate a whole new language that inclines more toward touch, toward the haptic. This is really because seeing is subscended by touching. It's not that seeing is *reducible* to touching, as if touching were more constantly present, the equivalent of a doubting Thomas thrusting his hand into the wound and feeling it for himself; it's that seeing, like hearing, is a part of touching, a whole that is not greater than the sum of its parts. The touch is lowly, susceptible, risky, humble—it subscends being able to see around and above and beyond a thing. It subscends because it is nearer, more intimate, quite the opposite of "more encompassing and less intimate."

Now we can think humankind without having to think "Mankind," and without having to imagine that there is no such thing as the human species or that differences between humans are superficial or irrelevant. We can talk about the human species while acknowledging difference because *humankind forms a subscendent whole*. There is an irreducible gap between little me and the human, but not because the human is ontologically greater than the sum of its parts. Humankind is not a negation of a human being, but rather an implosive whole that is susceptible to all kinds of phenomena. The Anthropocene is one of the first truly anti-anthropocentric concepts because via thinking the Anthropocene, we get to see the concept of "species" as it really is—species as a subscendent hyperobject, brittle and inconsistent. The Anthropocene is the moment at which humans come to recognize humankind, insofar as it subscends its parts (such as plastics and concretes in Earth's strata). The Anthropocene is the moment at which species as such becomes thinkable in a non-metaphysical way, such that humankind cannot rigidly exclude nonhumans. The human becomes visible as a species, that is to say, as a whole weirdly *smaller* than the sum of its (human, bacterial microbiome, prosthetic) parts. Humankind is, as I said before, intrinsically disabled without hope of a "healthy" (explosive) wholeness.

Spot the Hypocrite is the favorite game of the left, a product of the monotheistic holism we've inherited from Mesopotamia. In a world in which wholes are always bursting like spider's eggs into many, many parts, cynical distance cannot be achieved, because there is no place from which to grasp the totality without losing something. So, when it comes to a choice between Spot the Hypocrite or Burst the Spider Egg, we should be playing the latter game. A Google employee is capable of having critical, anti-Google thoughts. A bureaucrat in Soviet Lithuania is capable of having more-than-mixed feelings about what she's doing.

114

Theory class is intimidating, students are shy, participation is part of your grade, and so on. So, I say to them, "The dumber a question you ask, the higher a grade you will get." Children are well known for asking the most profound questions because these are the most simplistic: Why are you my dad? Do we have to have Wednesday? One teacher I like says, "Dare to be dumb." Some of us theory teachers could remember that a bit more when it comes to writing theory-style prose, no? It might be quite a relief if the questions became more profound and sound more dumb, and looked less sophisticated and intense. It might be more like what Socrates was aiming at, saying that he was just a clown, an *eirōn*, from which we derive our word *irony*. This isn't just a cute version of theoretical wonderment, setting the bar nice and low for intimidated students. This is the *actual* face of theoretical reflection, not just a dumbed-down version of it.

Maybe "dare to be dumb" is the whole thing, not just a way to get students to talk. There isn't a thin, bright line between true and false; we are, as Heidegger says, *always in the truth*. We're always in some form of Twittersphere, some Facebook post-y version of truth, like a fuzzy, record-store, his-idea-of-her-idea-of-their-idea of truth. Stephen Colbert's contribution to world peace comes in really handy here: truthiness.

Truth is haunted. Being true means feeling haunted. The confusion and ambiguity of truthiness space is intrinsic to truth, not some irritating grime that needs to be cleaned off. You never get to the naked, shining, transparent, perfect bit. Truth is always truthy because it always involves a way of being itself, a truth mode. Ideas always come bundled with ways of having those ideas. You can't have the idea without being in a certain mode. Ideas aren't colorless and flavorless. They have a specific frequency, a specific smell, they have ways of being thought.

There are truth prototypes. Many great artists talk in a proto-truth mode. Take Björk. Her song "Hyperballad" is a classic example: she shows you the wiring under the board of an emotion, the way a straightforward feeling such as "I love you" isn't straightforward at all. So, don't write a love song like that; write one that says you're sitting on top of this cliff, and that you're dropping bits and pieces off the edge like car parts, bottles and cutlery, all kinds of not-you nonhuman prosthetic bits that we take to be extensions of our totally integrated up-to-date shiny, religious, holistic selves; and then you picture throwing yourself off, and what would you look like—to the you who's watching you, who's still on the edge of the cliff—as you fell, and when you hit the bottom would you be alive or dead? Would you look awake or asleep? Would your eyes be closed or open?

My favorite version of "Hyperballad" is the Subtle Abuse mix, a twelve-inch remix, the expanded spectral dance version that has much more in it than just it, taking little bits of it and making thousands of copies of them, as if a whole were actually a bagful of eyes that on closer inspection were also bagsful of eyes, and so on, maybe down and down forever.

Twelve-inch remixes are neither copies nor separate things, but spectral bags full of eyes that haunt the seemingly individual house of a song. The DJ never weaves the twelve-inch vinyl discs into a seamless whole that's bigger than them. She weaves a whole lot of partial objects, eyeball bags into a large eyeball bag. A string of Pandora's jars adding up to one Pandora's jar, not one to rule them all, but a pretty good place for a night out.

When Björk asks you to remix her song she sends you all the parts, all the sound files, and says have at it. Do anything. Chop it into little pieces and multiply the pieces and rearrange them. Make more out of this than the whole that I made. Show me the wiring under the board of my showing people the wiring under the board. That's what she likes about it.

Now, in normal Western philosophy, namely agricultural-age religion version 2.0, starting with Aristotle, truth is something that comes in just one color: white. It is a matter of black and white. There can be no shades of gray. The Law of Noncontradiction rules, as does its niece, the Law of the Excluded Middle, which means that you can't have in-between categories. Which is too bad, really, because meadows and gorillas and humans and clouds and biosphere are just the things that you can't categorize as totally solidly themselves—meadows are made up of all kinds of things like grass and birds that aren't meadows, lifeforms are made up of all kinds of things that aren't alive; parts of the biosphere don't just go around being parts of the biosphere, they write poems and have sexual display and they irritate you when they beg for food and they make friends with goldfish in a pond.

The final version of a device subscends its prototypes and is not necessarily the truest one. It's the one that meets the needs of the firm. It's the one that meets the requirements of your ego, and it might not be the absolute best one. It is if you're lucky, if you're able to get out of your own way, as the best artists do. The official, black and white you is surrounded by this truthy proto-you, like a haunting halo, a much more expanded twelve-inch remix of yourself that you pretty much can't see. In neurological language, it's now called the adaptive unconscious, and in the philosophical tradition of phenomenology it's called style, and both of those declare that others can see much more of you than you can of yourself. This is how comedy works. A lot of comedy consists in portraying someone trying to do stuff from the position of who they think they are; but how they do it shows their total style, of which they are not in charge.

Björk allows wholes to be subscendent and this is different from ego display, which is where you think you can put a "This is a Tim Morton sentence" barcode on every letter and every bit of phoneme. Something about language shows you something about how meaning is also spectral. Being authentic doesn't really mean being totally and utterly something that transcends its parts. Being an author and being authentic in that sense aren't things we need to abolish or feel bad about or reduce to something else, because authorship already contains all kinds of other beings, a spectral, haunting otherness. A line of a Björk song doesn't shout "I love you" but instead shows you all the fuzzy little filigrees of wispy seaweed around and between and inside the "I" and the "love" and the "you."

Maybe black and white at the extremes don't exist at all. Heidegger claims that there isn't in fact a rigid, thin true–false separation. Not only does this mean that there is wiggle room for action, it also means that we don't have to keep playing the game of taking apart sacred cows if we want to be progressive philosophers. We can let wholes be wholes. We don't have to kill the author like Barthes said we should, because the author is already undead, a spectral, ghost-like being. We don't have to choose between big bad fascist *work* and open, ragged rhizomic *text*. We don't have to keep trying to find the right ism, the right access mode that performs our sophistication. The ecological age we are entering isn't going to be an artistic age of isms at all, because pimping one's access is grasping the wrong end of the Kantian stick. There's a VIP lounge of consumerism, just like there's a VIP lounge in every agricultural-age religion, where they tell you something more like the truth without the theistic or product-oriented copyright control. Indeed, consumerism is related to religion because the VIP lounge, called bohemianism or Romantic or reflexive consumerism, is about putting a spiritual value on experience itself, rather than on products.

We don't have to choose between incremental rearrangements of the deck chairs on the Titanic of the political and economic system, and some massive apocalyptic change of everything. We don't have to choose between life and death with a gun to our head, like hardcore pro-life arguments try to force us to. We don't have to cling for dear life to the idea that we should cling to things for dear life, aka our normal belief about belief, the one Richard Dawkins shares with fundamentalists, aka our normal idea of what the word "survive" means. We don't have to agree that the Buddhist idea of no-self means that you're just a bunch of atoms. What it means instead is that you are open. You are a haunted house. You contain gaps, voids, incomplete parts—like the universe according to Gnosticism.[6]

There exists a distorted idea of *author* which depends on an idea of *to possess* and the concept of *property*. We democratized agricultural-age religion so that now at least some people can be little gods. To do this, they have to own things, including themselves. There is some legal fine print here, to sever the spectral penumbra of style from the author, just like we've severed our ties with nonhumans both inside our bodies and outside, and inside our psychic bodies, and inside our philosophical and social systems. The very concept of *soul* is based on a severing and then a privatizing and then an abstracting of this form of specter, just as the concept of *the consumer* is the soul of little me, the guy who actually never demanded loads of plastic shrink-wrapping. In a way, it's better than agricultural-age tyranny and religion and stuff, but only because it has democratized tyranny. The net effect is that our version of the agricultural age is even more ecologically and psychologically violent. It's why we love previous versions of our Neolithic temporality, because it's like what Marx says about Greek art. It's like seeing pictures of yourself as a child, and there's something in your eyes that you don't see anymore.[7]

This is stuff some thought they had left behind, the stuff we call Paleolithic, the dreamtime space that is embarrassingly more like the world of Yoda. Why do we even want to watch *Star Wars*, which is about a genuinely non-theistic world where there is an ambiguous Force that surrounds and penetrates lifeforms and acts causally on them at a distance, without the need for mechanical touching? Why would that kind of topic even occur to someone and why would we flock in the billions to watch a film that portrays a crude, lame version of this concept? Because humans never actually severed their indigeneity to the symbiotic real, and this thing we keep telling ourselves with our words and our social space and our philosophy and our Stockholm syndrome feelings, that we are outside of that world, like Adam and Eve, is killing us and all life on this planet.

It's not even difficult to find that indigeneity again, because the VIP lounges have been containing it, because it's where the energy that powers the system lives, in what appears a distorted way to those not in the lounge, as the lounge is as tiny as possible and so the energy looks like a mere decorative afterthought. Take art or the aesthetic dimension in general. Some people think it's exactly this decorative afterthought, sometimes used as glue to stick the awful broken bits of black and white truth space, aka civilization, together in a fake way. But that's not being said from inside the VIP lounge: you are not supposed to speak from the lounge if you're a scholar.

ECOLOGICAL ECONOMICS: MULTIPLYING PLEASURES

With these lines the nonviolent direct action movement was born:

> Rise like lions after slumber
> In unvanquishable number
> . . .
> Ye are many! They are few!
> Percy Shelley, "The Mask of Anarchy"[8]

Shelley forgot to add: not just in an empirical sense having to do with bodies you can count, but in an *ontological* sense having to do with the structure of how things actually are. We are many all the way down, because we are wholes that are always less than the sum of their parts. We don't just combine into multitudes, we contain multitudes, as any self-respecting stomach bacterium will tell you.

We are many in the ontological sense too, and this implies that we can, should and will achieve solidarity with at least some nonhuman beings. The pathway toward this solidarity is about increasing and enhancing and differentiating more and more pleasures. This is quite different from the ecological task many of us assume is the right one: creating a restricted economy. Doing that would be a disastrous repetition of the oil economy, where concepts such as efficiency and sustainability (both perfectly anthropocentrically, not to mention neoliberally, scaled) have wreaked havoc on happiness, whether one is human or not. Talk of efficiency and sustainability are simply artifacts of the relentless use of fossil fuels. In a solar economy, you could have a disco in every single room of your house and way fewer lifeforms would suffer, perhaps vanishingly few, compared to the act of simply turning on the lights in an oil economy. You could have strobes and decks and lasers all day and night to your heart's content.

Economics is about how we organize enjoyment. As we begin to think about what ecological society would look like, we will begin to talk about how we organize enjoyment at the largest scales of our coexistence. An ecological society that doesn't put pleasure enhancement and diversification at its center is ecological in name only. The very concept of utility (as in an "electric utility," the American term for a power corporation) will need a serious upgrade. Happiness will no longer have *merely existing*—as opposed to *qualities of existing*—as its default, top level. The issue of how to live, the spiritual problem of reflexive consumerism, will become far more complex yet far less violent.

In a solar economy, the economic whole will subscend the parts. In an oil economy, oil subsumes everything in its explosive-holistic wake. In a solar economy, the question of who siphons and sells the solar power is a different type of question than the question of who owns the oil. In many more senses than we can now enact, humankind will have seized the productive forces, which is different from saying that nonhuman lifeforms will continue to be exploited. This is because humankind is a fuzzy, subscendent whole that includes and implies other lifeforms, as a part of the also subscendent symbiotic real.

4

Species

Men . . . begin, like every animal, by *eating, drinking,* . . . by . . . *actively behaving* . . . satisfying their needs. Start, then, with production.

—Karl Marx

Now we have a holism we can live with, an implosive, subscendent holism. Utilitarian holism, the holism of populations, is explosive—the whole is especially different (better or worse) than the part. There is no such thing as society! Or, specific people don't matter! Utilitarian holism sets up a zero-sum game between the actually existing lifeform and the population. One consequence is the trolley problem: it is better to kill one person tied to the tracks by diverting the trolley than it is to kill hundreds of people on the trolley who will go off a cliff if we don't divert the trolley. There's the left-wing variant: talk of wholes is necessarily violent (racist, sexist, homophobic, transphobic and so on) because what exists are highly differentiated beings that are radically incommensurable. In this leftist thought mode, there's as little chance of imagining you're a member of a group as in neoliberal ideology!

Gaian holism, the current ecological-political holism, also sets up a zero-sum game. An actually existing lifeform is a replaceable component. There is the right-wing version of this, often called Mother Nature. How dare we assume that we humans are more powerful than Mother Nature! If the Earth warms, Mother Nature will just replace her extinct parts. Then we have the correlationist versions of explosive holism. The Decider acts like population or Gaia, in a decidedly religious key. History, or progress, or destiny, gets to decide what's real. I had to run over you with this tank, it's the march of history. I may feel personally upset, but don't blame me, I'm just carrying out God's will.

As it approaches these sorts of whole, leftist thought rightly cringes. So ironically, it leaves out the one thing that could help it to think group political action!

Luckily, we've decided to be holists but to reject the explosive concept of the whole. Wholes are heaps whose members are uncountably undecidable. But they exist. A football team exists in the same way as a football player because it has a difference between what it is and how it appears: it might wear different uniforms at different matches. A whole is one, its members are more than one, so the whole is always less than the sum of its parts.

Species subscends me. Humankind exists, and I am a member of humankind. But there is so much more to me than being a member of humankind. So it's perfectly possible for us to achieve solidarity with nonhumans: I am not bound in an impervious whole and there are parts of me that also belong to other lifeforms, are common to them, or just are other lifeforms. We discover this solidarity down *below* the anthropocentric, murderous-suicidal idea of who we are. We are clouds, not metaphysically solid. You can't point to us directly, but we still exist. We are just as "poor in world" as the nonhuman beings that Heidegger labels that way, because "world" subscends its world parts. Being poor in world is what having a world means. There is no grand destiny to fulfill, thank goodness. The imperial anthropocentric project—a project with human as well as nonhuman victims—is over, because we can't think it anymore with a straight face.

To achieve non-racist, non-speciesist species, we need to allow heaps to exist. Vanilla logic doesn't allow for the possibility of heaps. If I have a heap, say a pile of sand, I can remove parts of it and still have the heap, and the same logic will apply until I only have one part left. So, there can't really be heaps. Or, I can add a grain of sand to another one, and there isn't a heap, and keep on going until I have tens of thousands of grains, and there still isn't a heap so there are really no heaps. Imagine an ecosystem, which is a heap of lifeforms. I can take the lifeforms away until there's nothing there, yet this paradoxical heap logic will still apply so that ecosystems can't really exist. Great! Let's build a mall! Fuck ecology! It doesn't make sense.

Humankind is a heap. If you care about ecology, you care about heaps, because lifeforms are heaps, and ecosystems are heaps. Heaps are paradoxical. Unless you allow for modal, paraconsistent and even dialetheic logics (that can say things are more or less true, or both true and false under some circumstances), you can't allow ecological beings to exist. No one human is responsible for global warming. Her use of fossil fuels to start the engine of her car is statistically meaningless. But a heap of car-startings—say, all the ones she does in her life, and all the other car-starters on Earth—do cause global warming! And yet, if we take one car-starting away, there is still a heap that causes global warming—and we can continue until there's just one key turning in one ignition, and the same logic applies. So, nothing causes global warming. To allow ecological beings such as ecosystems and global warming and humans and DNA to exist, we need to allow heaps to exist, and we need to allow heaps to be radically different from their members. Radically different.

There is a subscendent gap between humankind and its members. This means that for humankind to exist, sets that contain members that aren't strictly members of those sets must exist. We will upset Bertrand Russell, but we will have Cantor, Gödel and Turing cheering us on. Now we also know that ecological action only takes place at the heap level. Destroying or "saving" Earth is a matter of collectives.

What about all the species, the biosphere—the heap of heaps? The same logic works here. If we remove a heap, the heap of heaps is still a heap. So, heaps aren't real, and it doesn't matter that lifeforms go extinct—if we cling to a rigid true–false distinction and if truth means not contradicting yourself. So, the entire thing is also subscendent and is therefore vague and fuzzy. But this is great because it means that heaps can combine. I can be a member of one heap and a member of another heap at the same time. More than combining, heaps can overlap. There is no top level, no one heap to rule them all, so we have lost the idea of a one-size-fits-all political or economic structure. Communism cannot come in a one-communism-to-rule-them-all form, for instance, an official version imposed by the state. But we have gained the idea that heaps can be shared, which means that species can be symbiotic, which means that it's part of being a species to be able to have solidarity with other species. And because of the subscendent gap between a heap and its members, ecological action must be collective, so we can let our individual selves off the hook and stop preaching at each other.

HUMANS WITHOUT HUMANITY

So, it's perfectly possible to talk about species without resorting to universalist language that deletes, for instance, the obvious uneven distribution of responsibility for global warming.[1] We don't have to stay at the level of specific human groups, populations or cultures. We can talk about ourselves at a larger space-time scale, without compromising our politics. The Left had better be able to talk about humankind, because if we don't, we will have ceded that level of discussion to BP and Silicon Valley.

Subscendence is the half-sister of transcendence, which has to do with gaps between things and how they appear, gaps that can't be pointed out in ontic space-time. Whereas immanence, which is a very popular way of talking in an ecological way, eliminates these gaps. But if there is no difference between a polar bear and a polar bear appearance, then when the polar bear goes extinct, there is no problem. In fact, extinction doesn't really happen. Whereas, in a world of subscendence, extinction happens and I can think it, but

I can't know it or see it or touch it. Evolution, biosphere, global warming: all these are hyperobjects. They happen and I can think or compute them, and yet I can't directly see them. Evolution and the biosphere are telling us something about polar bears. They are also subscendent.

A symbiotic community—we are all symbiotic communities—is a perfect example of a subscendent whole. (Indeed, it would be better to call it a "symbiotic collective" for that reason.) I am less than an individual qua human with "This is a human being" engraved on every single piece of me. I am a human insofar as I have bacteria and prostheses such as cows and fossil fuels. Nothing is like a stick of Brighton rock, a tube of mint-flavored candy, usually white inside and pink outside, with something like "A present from Brighton" inscribed in pink all the way through the tube, so that however much you suck on it, the writing remains. But this is not how things are. To exist is to subscend one's parts. It's not that I don't exist, that my parts are more real than me. It's that I *faintly* exist. Likewise, humankind exists faintly. Thus, we *can* know ourselves because we don't set ourselves up as especially different, which would require another especially different being with whom to compare ourselves.[2]

One of the things disrupting our human world is . . . humankind.

Now we have a way to think what the myth of Adam Kadmon and Hobbes's Leviathan imagine in an explosive holist way: a body consisting of many bodies. Hobbes's support for monarchy arises from the explosive holism with which the whole is thought. But now we can think the body of humankind in an implosive way. A collective, rather than a community, is a faint subscendent whole. Now we can think humankind beyond sentimental reductionism to an explosive whole: "We're all in this together," "We are the world." Appeals to a universal humanity underlying appearances are politically dangerous.[3] The collective powers of humankind have been displaced onto concepts such as God, as Feuerbach argued, but also onto concepts such as Man and Humanity. The explosive concept of the human is a form of alienation.

A racist or a speciesist is someone who believes that one can point to species in ontic space-time. A subscendent humankind contains by contrast an irreducible gap between itself and little me. *Species* is *spectral,* and the human is a near-at-hand example of this spectrality. Communism is a specter not only because it frightens the capitalists, but also because it involves spectral beings who do and do not coincide with themselves at every point. It involves specters by allowing their full spectrality to manifest.

DOWN WITH NATURE, DOWN WITH ARTIFICE

Thinking this way about species permits us to resolve a debate within Marxist ideology theory, concerning whether or not there is such a thing as "human nature," the debate between Althusserians and non-Althusserians. Althusserians argue that there was an epistemological break between pre-*Capital* Marx and the Marx of *Capital* onward. The break consisted in dropping the idea of an essence from which humans have become alienated. The Althusserian view is that this very idea, that humans are separate in some sense from their contextual, economic enjoyment mode, is an *expression* of ideological alienation.

Let's summarize what I'm about to say in brief, and a bit schematically. Marx's non-Althusserian, pre-*Capital* alienation theory of ideology is *right, but for the wrong reasons.* And that's because there is indeed something that escapes the clutches of ideology, not because there's an intrinsic vanilla continuous substantial Nature underneath appearances—the Aristotelian essentialist version that the cool kids are right to be suspicious of—but because of OOO object withdrawal. And this in turn means that the stuff that differs from its appearance isn't just the human being, but also the brick, the Jim Henson puppet, Frank Oz's voice, goldfish and black Audis. Furthermore, the Althusserian theory—the post-"epistemological break" Marx of *Capital* who holds that ideology is all pervasive and has no outside, and so forth—is *wrong, for the right reasons.* Once again: good old alienation theory is right for the wrong reasons, and the cool kids' theory is wrong for the right reasons. The latter is the case, because it's true that you can't access the outside of your access mode, by definition; yet this doesn't mean that access modes and data are all there is. OOO is capable of resolving a decades-long, very technical debate within Marxist theory. Now let's go through this in greater detail.

The *content* of the non-Althusserian view is correct, but not for the stated reasons, in such a way that the *format* of the Althusserian view is wrong, but for the right reasons! What humans have become alienated from is humankind, an implosive whole that is a part of a similarly subscendent symbiotic real. But the way explosive holism expresses the belief that human being is a substance that underlies economic relations is itself a form of alienation.

The split between the Althusserian and non-Althusserian views maps onto the agrilogistic ontological split between appearing and being. For example, we might argue that alienation means that there is some original essence that is deprived of its full expression in capitalism. There is some constantly present substance that gets parceled out, frozen, segmented, diverted, reformatted. Underneath appearances, which for Marxism means underneath (human) economic relations, the song remains the same. This is commonly held to be the view of the early Marx. One argument for it is that if there is nothing underneath, how come we *feel* such suffering in capitalism?[4]

Such an argument raises an immediate objection: it's superimposing something we can *feel* on top of something *structural*. It *doesn't matter* whether we can feel alienated or not: we just are alienated, and feeling alienated isn't what alienation means. So, a variant of the non-Althusserian position is that humans are prevented from the full exercise of their productive powers; within capitalism only a limited range of pleasure modes are available, no matter how wide-ranging they seem. This is closer to what Marx means by species-being, which has to do with production or creativity. Production isn't about working on sheet metal in a factory, necessarily. Production is the pleasure of biting into a fresh juicy peach:

Men do not by any means begin by "finding themselves in this theoretical relationship to the *things of the outside world*." They begin, like every animal, by *eating, drinking*, etc., that is not by "finding themselves" in a relationship, but *actively behaving*, availing themselves of certain things of the outside world by action, and thus satisfying their needs. Start, then, with production.[5]

Notice that Marx uses the word "behave," the word we associate with bees executing algorithms and not with humans "acting."

Then there is the Althusserian view on the epistemological break between the early and the later Marx. The Marx of *Capital* and on isn't concerned with some original essence: there is none. Everything is produced (in the last instance), by (human) economic relations. The very idea that there is some original essence that has been betrayed is *precisely* the ideological form that alienation takes within capitalism. The idea that I am free to choose what I believe, as I feel free to choose my shampoo in a supermarket, is precisely ideology. The essence is a side-effect or byproduct of the enframing of reality by a certain mode of (human) economic relations.

Both the extreme correlationist and the vanilla essentialist arguments are holding two pieces of the Kantian puzzle, the thing in itself and how that thing appears. For the vanilla essentialist, the trouble has to do with how appearances are superficial, that there is an underlying essence that is unaffected by capital, and therefore alienated to the extent that it can't find expression. We are wage slaves who upon liberation will be fully ourselves, no longer slaves. We will be de-objectified. Liberation strips away *false appearances*.

For the correlationist essentialist, the picture is quite different. What is constantly present are (human) economic relations. The idea that there is a difference between real us and commodified us is the illusion. Liberation means that this illusion collapses. So, what remains is the freedom to posit whatever type of reality we want. Liberation strips away *false reality*.

Acknowledging humankind suggests another solution. We aren't totally caught in ideology, not because there is an underlying nature that is constantly present, but because of object withdrawal—because we are spectral beings. Yet in turn this means that interpellation is a deep feature of how things are. We are not capable of venturing outside of our access modes. We are shrink-wrapped in them, so that we anthropomorphize everything. But that doesn't mean that there's no outside at all, or that we are caught forever within anthropocentrism.

There's a big difference between saying that we anthropomorphize and that we are anthropocentric. Marx himself argues that we can't help anthropomorphizing. That's what species-being means. Things become realities for us when we bring them into economic relations. But this is not a prison without windows, because as I anthropomorphize this bunch of grapes, the grapes are grape-morphizing my fingers and my mouth, causing me to handle them just so. Anyone who has taken drugs will tell you that there is a more or less "right" way to handle them—one is drug-morphized. Everything is in the –morphizing business.

Let's revisit the question of bees and architects, and the difficulties of distinguishing rigorously between algorithms and people. This difficulty gives rise to a spectral realm in which personhood becomes uncanny—it's real in some sense yet we can't point to it directly. The fundamental problem with dancing tables is that I can't distinguish myself from one very rigorously, which doesn't mean I'm a table, and doesn't mean that the table is definitely a person. Science indicates that nonhumans might not simply execute algorithms. Ants hesitate—they circumspect when they climb up little ladders. Bees have mental maps to guide them home. Rats experience regret . . . The trouble is that this list of observations might be never-ending, since anthropocentrism could keep on refining what counts as a person so as to exclude any behavior of a nonhuman whatsoever—the tactic of proof-by-data invites this condescending delay.

We could, however, go the quick-and-dirty philosophical route, which has the benefit of being much more energy efficient and laying its cards on the table. Prove that *you* are imagining or acting rather than executing or behaving. Prove that your *concept* that you are imagining is not the very thing that humans have been programmed to picture about themselves! Like Descartes you will find there is no way out of this bind. Everything you can think concerning your personhood could be an artifact of being an android.

What are we to conclude from this? That you're not a person? Far from it. What we conclude is that our concept of *person* must be inaccurate. It is far too rigid and dogmatic. Perhaps people are cheaper than we like to think. Perhaps it's not so difficult to be a person, because *person* isn't quite as intense as all that. Not that there are no people, but that *person* is cheap. Lo and behold, we have just extended personhood to nonhuman beings, without discriminating between conscious and nonconscious, sentient and nonsentient—or for that matter alive and not-alive. *Person* is a spectral category that can apply to all such beings.

Far from thinking personhood as a special emergent property of special interactions of special algorithmic processes (or whatever), this way doesn't depend on reductionism at all. Strangely, cheap personhood is far more resistant to being reduced to atoms or brain firings than the expensive one! We don't need to specify that personhood emerges from states of matter (or organization of subsystems or what have you), or that personhood is some special extra fact (such as a soul) added mysteriously onto matter (the Cartesian solution). Personhood is a widely available (in fact, universally available) category, flimsy, subscendent and spectral. We have just admitted that *everything* might be a person. Part of this admission is that we are caught in the subjunctive mode that Descartes wants to collapse into the indicative. "I might be an android" is as unacceptable to him for its "might" as for its "android."

Such a thought process wants to eliminate doubt and paranoia. But what if doubt and paranoia were default to personhood? What if being concerned that I might not be a person were a basic condition of being one? This seems to be what the Turing test is pointing to. It's not that personhood is some mysterious property that we grant to beings under special circumstances, or that it doesn't exist at all except for in the eye of the beholder, or that it's an emergent property of special states of matter. It's that personhood now means "You are not a non-person."

In the UK, there is an urban myth about the legal definition of "not being in possession of yourself," aka "not being a person." Someone, such as a lawyer, needs to go beyond philosophical niceties and define, using some empirical signal, supposedly transcendental concepts such as *person*, something lawyers argue and argue about regarding, say, chimps in zoos.

The urban myth says so much about how we still regard being a (human) person as (paradoxically) the property of a subject (at the very least, this is an infinite regress and, of course, it's absolutely ecological violence enshrined in law) and as a mind in a body, with an unmentionable interface between them whose operation remains obscure. Legend holds that *if you have taken more than five hits of acid, you are not in possession of yourself and cannot testify in court.* Evidently there is a double standard here—chimps have on the whole done less than five hits of acid . . . There is an ontological assumption about chimps at work. There is an implicit acceptance that vague bundles of things can exist: otherwise the sorites logic would apply. One hit—still a person? Yes. Two hits? Yes. Three hits? Yes. You can keep adding hits to the person and the same logic will apply.

My flimsy yet significant, spectral being is well illustrated by the following fact, which we can demonstrate using arguments from utilitarianism. Ecological phenomena such as global warming and radiation last tens of thousands of years. Over that time span, the following will be true:

(1) No one will be meaningfully related to me.
(2) Every action I do now will have a greatly amplified significance.[6]

My effects on the world will have been immense. But I qua Tim Morton won't matter at all. My specific personhood has become ethically cheap, while the effects of my existence on other beings in the world have become supremely urgent. It is as if I have become a poltergeist, visible only in the shattered cups and weirdly opened doors I have left behind.

The "alienated essence," or non-Althusserian argument, is *right for the wrong reasons*. We have been alienated, but not from some consistent self-present essence. We have been alienated from spectral inconsistency. We have been Severed. The "nothing outside of ideology," or Althusserian, view is *wrong for the right reasons*. The human is indeed produced by language, discourse, correlation, economic relations and so on, such that there is nothing "behind" ideological appearances. But *there is something in front of appearances* (ontologically in front, not spatially), an inconsistent spectral essence we are calling humankind. Humankind is not despite appearance, nor produced by appearance. Humankind's essence is futurality, a not-yet quality that resides in front of how humankind appears—which is why we can't see it, *because we are it*. And this futurality is not special to humankind, but rather shared by coffee mugs, galaxies and trade unions.

We have generated a new theory of ideology. There is "nothing" under appearance, but not because appearance is all. Appearing is totally intertwined with being, and being withdraws. So, the appearance is always a distorted, low-amplitude rendition of the spectral X-powers of a being. What capitalism distorts is not an underlying substantial Nature or Humanity, but rather the "paranormal" energies of production.

ADVENTURES ON THE SPECTRAL PLAIN:
RACISM AND SPECIESISM

"This is my land, by definition, and I have the right to dispose of whatever else is on my land in whatever way I see fit." That "dispose of" should alert us to how the notion of private property is tied to the notion of liquidation. On this view, a landowner has the right to kill whatever lifeforms are on their property.

Which comes first, racism or anti-environmentalism? This has to do with a deep philosophical issue: which subtends the other, racism or speciesism? Does racism exist because we discriminate between humans and every other lifeform? Or does speciesism exist because we hold racist beliefs about people who don't look exactly like us?

Consider the fact of land ownership as republican qualification for voting rights in the eighteenth century. Voting rights were tied to slavery. Surely this phenomenon is part of the legacy of agrilogistics, and its construction of a caste system. The caste system distinguishes between humans; then the distinction is mapped onto nonhumans. The tendency to see nonhumans as unthinking and even unfeeling machines is predicated on the objectification and dehumanization of other humans, not the other way around. It is racist to suppose that some humans are degenerate, resembling apes for instance, not because apes really are degenerate. The degeneracy of the ape is a negative projection, not unlike the projection of positive human qualities "upwards" to a deity. The very concept of race as an ontically given reality, as in the anti-Darwinist racism of the biologist Louis Agassiz (his categories, such as "Caucasian," still grace some paperwork), is itself racist, and for this very reason: the idea that there are ontically different "races" as if there were different species. (This is drastically different from claiming that racism doesn't exist, as in the habitual right-wing blindness to the category of racism as such.)

The struggle against racism is exactly the struggle against speciesism, which is one of the ways maintenance of Nature works. Totalitarian and fascist societies can be weirdly ecological, in ways that disturb us about ecology: like eugenics, or animal rights (the Nazis were all over that), reforestation—think Lenin talking about putting loads of fertilizer in the soil. In the case of fascism, what is imagined to be the cause of the degradation of the people is what is held to be abject and uncanny, pathologically "unclean," and this politicized disgust surely does resonate with some kinds of ecological awareness: our symbiotic coexistence exceeds neat concepts of boundaries. The point, however, is that one can't get rid of the abject, "unclean" and uncanny beings without immense and escalating immunitary violence. This is obviously because symbiosis is not an optional extra: one cannot peel everything off or heal one's intrinsic brokenness, because the nonhuman being stuck to you is a possibility condition for your existence. With his moody ennui, Baudelaire shows how to tunnel down into deeper ecological awareness *underneath* fascism. Instead of trying to over-power the superman, we could slip out from underneath.

We make beings extermination-ready by designating them as uncanny, disturbingly not-unlike-us-enough beings that inhabit the Uncanny Valley. In robotics design, it is frequently said that as android designs approach close resemblance to humans, they enter the Uncanny Valley, populated at its nadir by the zombie, an animated corpse. At a certain point of closer resemblance, our identification with the android ceases to be uncanny.

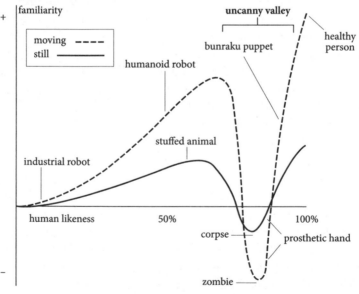

Figure 3. The Uncanny Valley (Masahiro Mori)

The Uncanny Valley concept explains racism, *and is itself racist* and, in addition, profoundly *ableist*. On one peak resides the so-called "healthy human being." On the opposite peak, waving to us cutely, are nonhuman beings who look *unlike* us enough not to provoke the uncanny reaction. R2-D2 and Hitler's dog Blondi are "over there" on the peak opposite us, the good, fascist "healthy human beings." Racism tries to forget the abject valley that enables this nice me-versus-nature, human-versus-nonhuman, subject-versus-object and health-versus-pathology setup to work. But these peaks are illusions, and there is no uncanny valley, because everything is uncanny, because we can't say for sure whether it's alive or not alive, sentient or not sentient, conscious or not conscious, and so on. Everything is spectral, undead, in unique and different ways. The Uncanny Valley flattens out into the *Spectral Plain*. Speciesism exists because humans can be differentiated decisively from nonhumans. And they can be because of racism: because the deep trough of the Uncanny Valley separates humans from puppies in a clean-seeming way, as long as we ignore the beings who have been thrown into the Valley of pathologized abjection. Speciesism depends on the dehumanization of some humans, with anti-Semitism as its template.[7]

Freud argues that the uncanny is keyed to realizing that we are embodied beings.[8] And what is more embodied than being a part of the symbiotic real? Doesn't the uncanniness of beings caught in the Uncanny Valley have to do with how they remind us of the non-manipulable, embodied, "less than human" aspect of ourselves, our very species-being? The struggle to have solidarity with life-forms is the struggle to include specters and spectrality. Without this, ecological philosophy falls into a gravity well where it becomes part of the autoimmunity machination just described.

Let's reverse engineer a concept from the Uncanny Valley. There's a phylogenetic part (the caste system is derived from agrilogistics), and there's an ontogenetic part (humanoids, hominids, hominins, primates and so on). The human body is a historical record of nonhuman evolution. Racism has to do with thinking one can point to certain physical features as indicators of the proper: it has to do with a metaphysics of presence and a substance ontology whereby one color is non-marked (it's not treated as a color but as the default quality of the substance, totally bland, "white").

The struggle against racism is thus also part of the de-anthropocentrization project. Whiteness, after all, is a direct artifact of the type of agricultural logistics that severed human–nonhuman ties. Wheat was farmed in areas in which it lost much of its nutritive value. At higher latitudes, wheat can't produce enough vitamin D to prevent humans from getting sick, unless humans become more efficient solar processors of the vitamin D in sunlight. Whiteness is therefore very recent and ecologically disastrous, since it was historically intertwined with speciesism. The program that brought us white bread also brought us whiteness as such.

5

Kindness

"What are you?" asked the little bird. "You are the same size as a giraffe and you have the same spots as a giraffe but you cannot BE a giraffe because you have such a short neck."

"I AM a giraffe, said Jeffrey, "but my neck has not grown. Because of this I can't play with other giraffes. I have no friends." And he began to cry.

"Do not cry," said the little bird. "I too have no friends. Let us go for a walk. My name is Peter."

"What are YOU?" asked Jeffrey. "You are the same size as a bird and you have the same wings as a bird but you cannot BE a bird because birds do not go for a walk. Birds FLY."

"I AM a bird," said Peter, sadly, "but I cannot fly. Because of this I can't play with other birds. That is why I'm lonely."

"My name is Jeffrey," said the giraffe. "Let's be friends and play games together. Climb on my back and we'll find somewhere to live."
—Frank Dickens, *Fly Away Peter*

Now it's time to investigate the last syllable of *humankind*.

Being kind is a political program rather than a greeting card, ethical injunction. *Kind* has to do with what we are. We have specific qualities—we are humans, not toasters—but in such a way that we can't abstract some bland (usually white, male) essence of "human" from the parts of being human. Being kind means being-in-solidarity with nonhumans: with *kind-red*. This includes acknowledging the spectral dimension of existence that is a necessary aspect of the symbiotic real.

To be a thing at all is to be different from how you appear, even to yourself, in a structural way. It's like what happens in film noir. The ultimate plot of a noir film is where the detective ends up chasing himself—not just someone *like* a self. But this chasing-of-oneself is exactly what happens in any first person narrative because the narrating *I* is structurally different from the *I* that is the topic of the narration.

This chasing-of-yourself is something that consumerism relies on. You define yourself via your products: I'm a Mac person, you are what you eat, she is an acid head, Toys R Us. Consumerism contains ecological chemicals, and this is one of them. It's about how consumerism makes "spiritual" experience into its top access mode. This mode has gradually colonized all the others, so that now we are all experience junkies, just like a handful of avant-garde Romantic-period poets. We are all about style, not fashion; surfing, not buying a specific thing; window shopping; browsing; scrolling through our timelines.

As we style ourselves according to our products and our thingies, something else is happening. We are being styled by them. Without doubt, this is what we are told is disturbing about consumerism— Coca-Cola is controlling your head, we have become mindless pod people . . . But when you think about it, this is a narrow, distorted version of relating to a nonhuman being without discriminating as to whether it's alive or dead, sentient or nonsentient, conscious or nonconscious: an *aesthetic* mode of relating. And it's about allowing that thing to relate to us. Coca-Cola controlling your head is only horrible if you think you are the only form of being that has a head to control.

All this is tantamount to saying that we need a new theory of acting. (Later on, I'm going to call it "rocking.") We have a disastrous fear of passivity. What if passivity were not the opposite of activity, like black versus white, but a way of thinking a spectral version of activity? We would be freed from having to debate endlessly whether a chimp can *act* rather than simply *behave*, before we can allow it out of the prison of the zoo. What needs to be shown is that chimpanzees and humans are not mere machines, but we can't prove anyone can act. It's easier to show that chimpanzees and humans are both *spectral*. Reductionism wants to erase the whole thing, but this is just an upside-down way of retweeting agricultural-age religion. Reductionism wants to eliminate the possibility of finding anything outside the narrow bandwidth of beings already defined as people. It's not surprising that the current state of agricultural society has spawned the most violent version yet, called eliminative materialism. What really needs to happen is that we need to get to a place that when we hear the word "materialism," we don't hear the words "reduce" or "eliminate."

Style exceeds intentions. A character trying not to execute their style is funny because, as Stirner observes, "toil[ing] to get away from [oneself]" is what one can't do.[1] As I asserted earlier, much comedy is based on this dilemma. Style as such is species-being, a non-intended, "nonhuman" and unconscious aspect of ourselves. If humankind exists, then humankind has a style: *being kind*.

Consumer products are a place where nonhumans are found inside social space, which means that social space was never exclusively human. Consumer products are made from the symbiotic real: they act as an interface between human reality and the symbiotic real. Consumer products count as nonhuman beings in their own right. It's simply a matter of the amount of nonhuman styling of ourselves to which we are susceptible; nonhumans constantly impinge on our world. This isn't a matter of taking a vacation in someone else's misery. We can visit the trash can for a bunch of discarded flowers. What we are talking about is acknowledging this always-already quality of nonhuman impingement, and bringing that awareness, which is not the opposite of action but rather a quantum of action (as I will show), into actions at other scales. This acknowledgment is a matter of more or less, not of black and white. It is quantitative and analogue rather than qualitative or binary. Acknowledgment includes the deliberate forging of links between humans and nonhumans, based on our acknowledgment that we share their worlds, and they share ours. This is also a matter of modality, not of all or nothing.

Let us now define *kindness* as acknowledgment of nonhumans in the terms I just described, whether acknowledgment is in its quantum or ground state (what is conventionally called "aesthetic experience"), or whether acknowledgment is in its more classical state (what is conventionally called "ethical or political action"). Again, we are going to need to modify "active" and "passive." Forging solidarity links is a matter of always already having been caught in the general solidarity mode of the symbiotic real.

Acknowledging ourselves to be –morphized by a nonhuman means acknowledging that the nonhuman is sharing its world with us. As we saw earlier, sharing worlds is modal: we can share 20 percent of a spider's world, and so on. As we let more and more in, we exit normal consumer space. It's as simple as that. Or at least as simple-sounding as that, which is a good start. This is the flip side of the Kantian idea that rules our world: that we are in a loop with data or appearances or whatever. The flip side speaks to the fact that this is happening at the same time as the actual thing in itself is withdrawn from our access modes, whether they are perceiving or thinking-about or licking or hammering or folding . . .

Access modes are modes of pleasure. The realms of access are necessarily limited by object withdrawal, and consumerism has a determinate shape to it—it's a set of *these* but not *those* performance styles. There must be pleasure modes that can't be co-opted, yet we can only discover them by embracing consumer pleasure modes that "say" something true, namely that access is in a loop with what is being accessed—a loop commonly referred to as *desire* rather than as *need*.

As well as the active–passive binary, another binary we will need to address if we are going to achieve solidarity with nonhumans, to live up to our kindness, is the need–desire binary. Need is always posited with respect to the past, as in the exclamation "I needed that!" Or need can simply express very strong desire: "I so need to have sex right now." Needs are desires that have been actualized or abstracted in some way so that they stand over against us. Just as the realm of the commodity form abstracts labor into homogeneous abstract labor time, so some kind of realm abstracts desire into its alienated form, homogeneous abstract desire, otherwise known as need. Need is not in effect in the symbiotic real. For instance, there is no off-switch in the brain for salt. Who knows how much sodium each cell will require to maintain the back-and-forth of its chemical messaging via the sodium and potassium ion channels? "You need x amount of salt," is a distorted way of saying "The amount $x + n$ of salt will, in the long run, harm you by causing a major malfunction such as a stroke." "You need substance A or B in order to live," is a circular sentence, and an expression of alienated desire, akin to "You need to work to live." In truth, you live to eat salt. You eat salt until you die.

Unfortunately, the strongly reinforced meme of need versus desire, which also affects Marxist theory ("To each according to his needs"), is an artifact of agrilogistic computation. The concept of use-value as need must be dropped. The story goes that first we needed things, we knew what we wanted and we wanted what we knew—this was called "need" and need was transparent to us. Then came the Fall (or a Fortunate Fall), and we exited the Garden of Needing and entered the Desert of Desire, which was bad because we were thrown into loops and what we needed no longer coincided with what we wanted; or it was good for the same reason, because then the horizons of our worlds expanded. Thinking kindness requires that we drop the illusion of some unsullied "straight" need that got twisted into desire. We have to go all the way through desire, which in conventional Marxist terms means traversing the alienation of the commodity form rather than trying to return to a natural state posited as chronologically or logically prior to that alienation. OOO provides a very elegant reason for this. It has to do with the fact that what we are is the future, and how we appear is the past. It is our *futural* being that has been alienated, not our past.

Pleasure modes in excess of consumerism will definitely be found in the regions and edges where humans and nonhumans touch in all sorts of ways, social, psychic, philosophical, and physical. This is because consumerism is anthropocentrically scaled; when you get really close to a thing, it stops being anthropocentrically functional and thus ceases to be functional for consumerism. The revolutionary cry is not that consumerism gives us too much pleasure, but rather that *consumerism isn't enough pleasure*; we desire a lot more than that.

The loop form of consumerism, like the capitalism that happily demystifies the sacred cows, puts to death the prejudice that we can achieve escape velocity from phenomenological style, or for that matter from the symbiotic real. This is tantamount to arguing that a pure metalanguage is impossible. The thought lineage from Cantor through Gödel and Turing shows this to be the case. So does a simple logical analysis of metalanguage as such, a concept developed by Alfred Tarski early in the twentieth century, developed so as to avoid awkward, that is to say, loop-like self-referential or recursive sentences such as "This sentence is false." You can make a rule such as "'This sentence is false' is not a sentence." But I can make a virus that worms its way into that rule and infects it, such as "This is not a sentence." That makes the very idea of being a sentence, which the rule requires, into something contradictory.

Desire operates exactly like "This sentence is false." What Schopenhauer says about will—you can't desire to exit from desire—is what we are saying about consumerist possibility space.

Strong correlationist consumer ideology suggests that we float above consumerism like shoppers in a supermarket, waiting to select a style just as, according to Hobbes and Rousseau, "primitive" humans waited and then decided to enter into a social contract. But this is exactly what *can't* happen. Romantic consumerist spirituality is precisely not that, but a sliding-down *into* things (as in the phrase, "get into it"), where irony moves downward, not upward. The top access mode of consumerism is subscendent. I am now going to stop calling it the "top" for that reason and call it "the main key signature." Other key signatures may manifest within consumerist possibility space, but the main key signature is the spiritual consumerism of experiences. The idea that we are alienated because we float around like ghosts, not knowing what we want or why we want it, is exactly wrong. This floating is good!

The precise way that consumerism keeps on co-opting things is in the region of the very force that will help to unwind it. The endless game of trying not to sell out is not the pathway. But this is not because there is no authentic stuff despite consumerism. It's because our definition of *authentic* can no longer have to do with coinciding with oneself so that one can for instance float above one's embodiment, or maintain a firm grip on one's style, a grip that performs *sober* rather than *addicted*.

FASCINATION

Kindness means including nonhumans in our social designs, not because it's nice or because we need to condescend to things and make them ersatz humans with rights. Not for any reason involving good or evil at all, because that's an artifact of agricultural-age religion. We need to include nonhumans because it's *fascinating*. Because we can't help it. Because we know too much. We're not trying to *be* kind. It's that this is our kindness in the sense that this is how we are. We want to be maximum chameleons. Consider designing a house. We want our own use of our own house to be affected by how frogs and lizards and dust use it. It already is, in any case. There are all kinds of filters and air conditioners and mildew-resistant paint to eliminate nonhumans. You just have to imagine an upside-down version of that. Not that you are going to make a house that's going to kill humans; then the humans wouldn't be around to relate to the nonhumans.

The fascinating is one of two aspects of the numinous, along with the tremendous: the fear-inducing or awe-inspiring. The numinous is a displacement of human-kindness into a lordly, divine dimension. The capacity to be fascinated by the numinous is aesthetic appreciation restored to its wider-bandwidth, subscendent version, the one fringed with an aura of the sexual and erotic, with disgust, or horror, or excess. Our capacity for fascination is what fuels solidarity, not some pre-theoretical, prefabricated concept of need. Fascination is the aesthetic gravitational pull of entities toward one another, the dynamics of solidarity, within a forcefield-like matrix of sensitivities.[2]

Human-kindness goes beyond tolerance, which is based on an emotional economy of need, to appreciation, appreciation for no reason, based on an emotional economy of desire. This entails the possibility not of refraining from pleasure (which is simply displaced pleasure, or pleasurable restraint as such), but of allowing other beings to have pleasure. For some reason, this part of your house is where sparrows, not you, get to have fun. But you get to have fun by appreciating the sparrow fun. You become fascinated by enhancing and expanding nonhuman pleasure modes. In this way, vegetarianism (for example) is not about opposing cruelty or minimizing suffering or enhancing one's health by returning to a more natural way of eating, but about a pleasure mode designed to maintain or enhance the pleasure modes of pigs or cows or sheep and so on. The point would not be to create a society where pigs no longer existed, but one in which actually existing pigs get to enjoy themselves more, to go about their piggy business. Motivations for ecological ethics and politics can no longer be trapped in theistic discourses of good and evil, or biopolitical discourses of sickness and health, or petrocultural discourses of efficiency and sustainability.

Being—being a rock or a lizard, not just a human—means being a chameleon who picks up impressions of every surface she touches. That's the definition of genius that Keats likes; it's why he says Shakespeare is brilliant, because he can allow himself to be taken over by so many types of people.[3] Kindness means being kinda-sorta, because one is permeated with other beings, physically and experientially and everything else. When people use that word to discriminate—that they don't like your *kind*, for example—they are restricting it to the narrow bandwidth-ness that we have been exploring, the one that associates the word "kind" with the word "nature, "thus eliminating the shades-of-gray qualities of kind. We need both, at which point nature stops being nature underneath appearances, and appearances stop being superficial candy on top of nature.

As we open up the bandwidth of our experiences of thing data, we will inevitably reach a point that can't be co-opted or turned into a product at all. In my view, to be a thing is to be finite, and this must also apply to capitalism. We can overcome this finitude with a twelve-inch remix of consumerism, which is equivalent to allowing ourselves to be haunted by things. This is what achieving solidarity with nonhuman beings really looks like. It's like figuring out that one is also a specter in a haunted house of illusions and specters. One isn't there to demystify the ghost anymore, because this type of ghost isn't on a mission to steal money or make people unhappy. This type of ghost is just how things are, when you stop retweeting the agricultural-age religion that is gumming up our ways of imagining a different future.

We should pray to be haunted.

WE ARE THEM

What is the quantum of being haunted, of fascinated appreciation, of acknowledgment? What, to adapt Einstein, is the quantum of spooky *passion* at a distance? There is so little pleasure in the world of Christopher Nolan's *Interstellar*.[4] The drastic curtailment of pleasure is obviously one of the subplots: in effect, the protagonist, Cooper, is prepared to fall into a black hole in a foreign galaxy in order for his colleague, Amelia Brand, to go on a blind date on another planet with the particle physicist Wolf Edmunds, who for all we know might already be dead. The dilemma is the difficulty of locating even one droplet of pleasure in such circumstances, because that would mean one was able to act in the knowledge born from large-scale planetary awareness, negative awareness of humankind. So, this film can give us a clue. The basic problem the movie explores is this: You should save the world. But how do you *want* to?

Interstellar isn't really about leaving Earth. It's about how to restart our ability to imagine who we are, crushed by current social conditions and the shock of the Anthropocene. A question of how to open up futurality at a moment in which totally reified Nature, as the past, is weighing all lifeforms down like a nightmare. In particular, *Interstellar* allows us to think species very differently, to detach ourselves from the destructive idea of survival, which (as the film makes clear) is murder-suicide at a planetary level, and deeply intertwined with neoliberalism. Detaching from survival may look extreme, like allowing yourself to fall into a black hole.

In some indeterminate future—the indeterminacy itself is significant because its vagueness suggests how evacuated time has become—humans have resorted to farming ever-larger quantities of corn in order to survive an ecological catastrophe. The catastrophe is never spelled out but global warming is the obvious referent. Cooper is a corn farmer, an ex-NASA pilot and an engineer, who lives with his teenage son Tom and ten-year-old daughter Murph, and their grandfather Donald, his father-in-law; his wife is dead, and Cooper's ongoing grief is highly visible in the wedding ring still attached to his finger.

But this is only a tiny sliver of the grief that weighs down the characters, since the ecological catastrophe is claiming more and more of their lifeworld. We learn that crops are blighted with a fungus that will kill all food supplies and slowly increase the amount of nitrogen in the atmosphere until all humans go extinct. What is suggested in response is drastic. NASA's head physicist, Professor Brand, declares, "We're not meant to save the world. We're meant to leave it." So what am I, an ecological philosopher, doing promoting this dangerous propaganda? That's the interesting thing. The way the "leaving Earth" scenario plays out is strangely ecological.

Early in the film, Donald points out their neighbor farmer, who is burning his blighted crop—"They're saying it's the last harvest for okra. Ever." A few moments later, Cooper and Donald share a beer on the front porch. Donald chastises Cooper for still harboring dreams of space travel. Cooper replies: "We used to look up and wonder at our place in the stars. Now we just look down and worry about our place in the dirt." His daughter Murph has just been suspended for fighting her schoolmates over a censored astronomy textbook claiming the USA faked the moon landings to bankrupt the Soviet Union. "We don't need more engineers. We didn't run out of television screens and planes, we ran out of food. The world needs farmers," says the principal. "Uneducated farmers," replies Cooper without missing a beat. Being able to imagine something different than the world around is linked to freedom from oppression. So far, so Enlightenment. Education is part of the struggle, but not all of it. We require solidarity. How do we get there? Does the film help us?

Interstellar is a movie about genres: the question of what kind of world we want to inhabit is the question of what kind of art we want. "What kind of sci-fi movie is this anyway?" you think, as you watch the first half an hour. One of the powerful things about *Interstellar* is how futuristic Earth *doesn't* look. It looks as if things have regressed to a *Little House on the Prairie* level: you'd never know we were possibly a century or even two into the future. There is farmland, baseball, front porches, trucks. There are snippets of interviews from survivors of the Dust Bowl of the 1930s, from the documentary by Ken Burns, seamlessly woven in.[5] This makes a very powerful point: what is most futuristic is to observe the *continuity* between ourselves and all other agrilogistic eras. It's futuristic because thinking the contours of this continuity is part of how to exit from it: you have to figure out what form of prison you are in before you can escape.

Nonhumans are significant in their absence. Well, there *are* human-made nonhumans. There are robots, nonhumans simulating humans and adding to their powers, while remaining firmly on the yonder side of the Uncanny Valley: they look like gigantic metal packets of cigarettes. Apart from stultifying oceans of corn, there are no insects, no birds, not even a flower. There's hardly anyone else to have solidarity with at all. All the food is a corn derivative: fritters, bread, corn on the cob . . . This is monoculture taken to the limit. None of the habitable planets the NASA team visits in order to find somewhere capable of housing humans seems to have any actual lifeforms on it; at best, there are "organics," carbon compounds that might provide the buildings blocks for life. And they are "monocultures" of imagery: there is a wave planet and an ice planet (and both of them were shot in Iceland). This film is about living in extremis, and if you haven't already realized that the temporality *Interstellar* is pointing to is *right now*, then you need to think a bit before reading on. It's *we* who live in a world disconnected from other terrestrial lifeforms. We are causing mass extinction. The space program as conceived by NASA is a symptom of that continuity, as a feature of the Cold War between competing agrilogistic structures: capitalism and Soviet communism. And space is still seen as yet another frontier for pioneers. Cooper's Texan drawl (he is played by Matthew McConaughey) and his farming career, let alone his work for NASA, seem to emphasize this connection.

FROM GRAVITY TO LEVITY

Is there any wiggle room in the deathly "reality"-enforcing aesthetic environment of *Interstellar*? Despite all the indications to the contrary, the film does locate it, in the teeth of the machination that got humankind to the brink of extinction. And this is the point. We are not finished; there is still some hope, a tactic with which to begin to extricate ourselves and other lifeforms from the ecological catastrophe.

The five-dimensional beings who save humans are, of course, future humans. We could read this as an Oedipal "we came from ourselves," which hardly sounds very ecological. Lévi-Strauss's claim that myth computes chthonic origins (we came from others) versus autochthony (we came from ourselves) sounds very strange given that it's quite clear that we came from the symbiotic real. We came not exactly from ourselves nor from others but from *otherness*, from spectrality. Or, we could read the film as an allegory about how human experience subscends its empirical constraints. On this interpretation we are "saved" by restoring to ourselves a sense of the futurality that ecological panic and pain—let alone ecological policies and planning (ironically)—have crushed.

On another level, *Interstellar* is about going to the movies and allowing yourself to be overwhelmed and fascinated, allowing yourself to *visualize* as opposed to *see*. The five-dimensional future humans (the spectral "Them") have created a wormhole near Saturn. When Cooper asks where the wormhole leads, Professor Brand intones, "Another galaxy." One instantly wonders whether the movie they are all about to go and see is *Star Wars*, with its escapist "A long time ago in a galaxy far, far away." This is one instance in which escapism is politically charged within the film, and in a good way, because the "long time ago" and "galaxy far, far away" are indicated as aspects of humankindness as such, in a Feuerbachian sense, that have merely been displaced. Alienation is what makes them seem far away and long ago. The superpowers of humankindness are not natural or primitive, but futural.

If the movie we are supposed to visualize with reference to "another galaxy" is *Star Wars*, then we're talking about gravitating from a Christian-Neolithic view to a pagan, non-Neolithic one. It's very significant, since *Interstellar* is positioned as the hard sci-fi anti–*Star Wars*, employing an actual astrophysicist (Kip Thorne of Caltech) to generate real astrophysical equations to aid its astronomical realism, and so on. There are three glaring exceptions: the fantasy machinery that actually transports the crew from the world that's dying to the futural world(s); the wormhole, which is straight out of *Star Wars*; and the even more vivid example of "bent space," the five-dimensional "tesseract" inside the black hole that Cooper falls into. The golden wormhole is surely an inverted echo of the silver-blue hyperspace tunnel of Millennium Falcon fame. It's wrong to only either accept how *Interstellar* talks about itself as hard sci-fi, or to mock its use of fantasy elements. What's fascinating is that the film opens up a literal passageway from one kind of space to the other, from the realm of engineering to the realm of dreamtime.

The wormhole and its filmic cousins (Murph's room, the tesseract within the black hole and its seemingly inviolable fourth walls, its cinema-screen-like separation of past and present) are the reverse of Plato's cave, another form of cinema. Plato's character can't wait to get out of the cave to see the truth. In *Interstellar*, the truth lies *within* the cinema cave, the image for which keeps amplifying and amplifying as the film proceeds. The ship Endurance is one kind of cave. The wormhole is the pivotal instance: it floats in space like a gigantic crystal ball, as if we were able to see a dreaming mind, a mind full of other stars and planets. The black hole Gargantua is the most extreme, containing within it the tesseract in which Cooper witnesses, as if stuck watching a multidimensional film loop in hell, himself abandoning his daughter over and over again. From inside the black hole, no information can get out. Cooper's buddy, the elder-brother-like robot TARS, who as stated above resembles a two-and-a-half-meter-high silver packet of cigarettes, detects the "quantum data" that would reconcile gravity with the quantum theory of the other three fundamental forces of the universe, but he can't communicate it to Earth. In a practical sense, you can't get there (enhanced superpowers of humankindness, affiliation with nonhumans) from here ("sustainable," "efficient" production in the deadly name of Life).

Thus, *Interstellar* poses a political problem of interpretation and communication: how to tell you about this dream, how to tell you about this poem. You can't talk to the characters in the movie or the guy in the mirror or to the images in the poem. There is an ontological firewall. In *Interstellar* this is shown as a variant of the nightmare where you are screaming without being heard by someone right next to you. And like in a film or a poem, what you are seeing while trapped in the tesseract is literally the past, and you can't quite change it, not at least in the naïve way you want to.

When you dream, "All you can do is record and observe," as the astronaut Doyle says to Cooper in the wormhole when Cooper struggles to work his equipment in five-dimensional space. Action is as it were reduced to its *ground state*, the basic quantum state of a thing (when isolated and cooled close to absolute zero). At the ground state, the quantized particles of action turn out to be fascinated appreciation, as we will see.

Grief work is also a political project, and some societies (such as the indigenous one in Burkina Faso) are built around it. Grief work could be thought of as allowing yourself to dream in a futural way, rather than being caught in the deadly round of PTSD repetition. This repetitive machination is enacted in the symbiotic real by agrilogistic human social space, reacting to its own foundational principle, the Severing.

How to dream ecological awareness: dreams are futural as well as pictures of the past because they can be interpreted infinitely (let alone the paranormal possibility of predictive dreams). This dreaming can be contrasted with the current modes of ecological information delivery, which are aggressive and apocalyptic. Instead of traumatizing you with sheer data, the question is how to find patterns and how to doodle associations. The tactic is how to include not just prediction and accounting for things, but spectral, open *futurality* in our ethical and political decisions, the chameleon aspect of humankindness.

This devolves into the question of social utility, which is discussed in *Interstellar* with respect to love. Astronaut and biologist Amelia Brand makes the excellent point, against Cooper's devil's advocacy of the utilitarian-evolutionary benefits of loving, that "We love people who have died—where's the social utility in that?" For that matter, we love characters in novels and films, characters from the past who never existed (in a way, they are doubly dead). In a world in which the pursuit of survival has become so clearly fatal, this dimension-crossing capacity of love, dreams, and art is where the true ecological chemistry lies. Gravity, which plays a central role in the film (to get millions of humans off Earth will require anti-gravity and an understanding of how gravity works that is beyond our current knowledge), is depicted not as omni-present, instantaneous, omnipotent Neoplatonic Newtonian love but as risky, futural Einsteinian love, finite (howsoever gigantic) ripples and distortions of space-time.

At the very end, the humans on Earth have mastered gravity, thanks to Murph (who has grown up into a brilliant quantum theorist), who reads her father's gift of the watch correctly. How? Cooper manages to violate the fourth wall in the tesseract to reach his daughter as a child in one specific way: he is able to pull strings of gravity, as if they were puppet strings. Everything on Murph's side of the fourth wall (divided from Cooper's side by the book-shelves in her bedroom) is tied to tiny, translucent gravity strings. Cooper manipulates the watch like a puppet master so that the watch doesn't move forward in linear fashion, as watches normally do in the measurement of linear anthropocentric time. Now the second hand quivers and oscillates back and forth: it *rocks* (I shall soon explain the definition of rocking as the quantum of action).

Moreover, Cooper has become a poltergeist, a telekinetic ghost, making books and the second hands on watches dance in the way Marx thinks is less absurd than getting them to compute capitalist value. Cooper is also a specter from the future. In the denouement scene, Murph notices the second hand quivering in the narrative present, which the film has transformed into spectral nowness. This is because what we are watching is two streams of time juxta-posed, exactly like how a thing is a junction where past and future slide over one another. We see Murph the child sadly placing the watch, a souvenir her father gave her before his voyage through the wormhole, on the bookshelf where she earlier observed the books spelling out the word "STAY" in Morse Code. We see Cooper, floating in the black hole at the climax of the film, pulling the gravitational puppet strings. The present time of the narrative

seems to flow and float as adult Murph wanders around her childhood bedroom trying to figure out the message she realizes her
father had sent her from inside the tesseract when she was a child,
haphazardly picking up the watch while her brother returns irate
from a burning field and her boyfriend hustles the brother's wife
and kids into a truck. The denouement reveals the film itself as an
OOO object, a quivering nowness, a weird floating stillness where
Murph hesitates and the field burns and the angry brother is
coming in his truck, a still nowness made literally from overlapping streams of past film and future film.

We live in a world in which the past is trying as hard as possible
to eat the future as efficiently as possible. Every year the past gets
better at eating the future. Keeping the future open, refocusing
humankind on the specter of futurality: this is a key task of ecological politics. The ecological future is not about sustainability or
efficiency, for example. Petroculture dictates these terms, whether
the left or the right articulates them.[6] Gasoline is a precious, toxic
resource, made of the past, a fossil fuel. By burning millions of
years of the past of the symbiotic real in a few decades, humankind
has deleted the futurality of the future. If there is only the idea that
things could be different, futurality has become a tiny sliver, as
slender as the second hand of a wristwatch. Deletion has occurred
in the name of a present that has become reified and that now
stands over against the humankind that generated it. Species-being
as such is threatened, the nonhuman sucker that connects humankind to the symbiotic real. Nothing could be as inconvenient for
the expression of species-being than its total erasure.

Extinction is the logical conclusion of alienation, not a
biological fact outside of alienation possibility space but its
furthest limit. Extinction is even less visible than personal death.
"Last man" narratives, of which *Interstellar* has a slight flavor, are
fantasies of being able to witness extinction. But this is exactly
what won't happen, as is easy to realize: no one will be around to
write a news headline about the extinction of humankind.
"World without us" narratives that enjoy how Gaia or nature

will return after humankind goes extinct are dangerously ideological last-man fantasies, where the reader or viewer occupies
the privileged, anthropocentric position of the last man. The
fantasy is that the observer can see themselves as an ingredient at
the same time. The correlator and the correlatee fuse in an
impossible synthesis. But what is in fact the case is that *observing
just is a mode in which the ingredient executes itself.* Observing is
what humankind does. So, we aren't in fact "seeing" anything
but simply *intuiting our objecthood* in the OOO sense through
the porous barrier between dimensions that are not thought
as incommensurable, solid, smoothly functioning worlds.
Seeing believes itself to be its own ground, and what it sees are
the dualisms of subject–object, human–nonhuman, conscious–
nonconscious, sentient–nonsentient, lifeform–non-life, thing–
nothing. Each term in the binary is just a reification.

Think about that: *anthropocentrism is directly opposed to the interests of humankind.* Moreover, humankind is now so chemically
entangled with other lifeforms that going extinct means either that
a vast number of lifeforms will have already gone extinct, or that
they are about to go extinct. The world without us is at best a very
severely damaged symbiotic real, whose pleasure possibilities have
been drastically curtailed.

When an opera singer's voice fuses perfectly with a glass, the
glass becomes fragments of shattered glass. Beauty is a moment of
stillness that announces this possibility. The telepathic mind-meld
between the beautiful thing and the experiencer is like a tiny death
signal. Part of the allure of beauty is that it announces the fact of
fragility, that to be requires a flaw that will eventually undo the
being. As goth culture intuits, beauty is death in a very low-dosage
format, like a vaccine. A little bit of poison is quite good for you,
as anyone who has tried to avoid the taste of bitterness (a poison
signal), eaten too much McDonalds, and almost died of a heart
attack can tell you. Beauty is an exquisite droplet of poison.

The "world without us" ideology, a drastic version of the last-
man fantasy where the last man is the viewer of the narrative, is a

sadistic fantasy that increases the poison droplet until it is neither beautiful nor safe. From the pseudo-safety of the dramatic or narrative fourth wall, we rubberneck a simulation of rubbernecking the death of the symbiotic real.

"We brought ourselves." When he says that, Cooper begins to reason in spectral fashion about what will have been the case, that humankind somehow finds the ability to execute its species-being in five dimensions. The visual and narrative logic of *Interstellar* makes it clear that this ability has nothing to do with Oedipal bootstrapping or any other "if it's depressing it must be true" explanations. This has nothing to do with a phallogocentric guarantor, a god outside of time and space and language. The 5-D beings are figures for human spectral superpowers, our pre-Severing still-intact species-being, our spirit animals and animal spirits. The nonhumans that surround, penetrate and support us, that are us and are not us, the fuzzy cloud of nonhumans that constitutes humankind, are the "extra dimensions" that can be glimpsed out of the corner of our correlationist eye, never totally invisible, capable of being inferred even from within anthropocentrism, as in Cantor's diagonal proof of another dimension of number. "They" still signal to us. And *one of Them is humankind as such*. Humankind intuits its objecthood in the OOO sense. We are still intact. We're just in shock, and we've been shocking ourselves for thousands of years. "Dark ecology" is how we find ourselves in a story we have written, and the next part is becoming conscious authors of the story we are writing. It has nothing to do with mastery or cynical distance or agrilogistics in space— Cooper dislikes intensely what the humans have done with his quantum data, namely to reproduce the toxic farm model in a gigantic spacecraft.

Contrast this helpful ambiguity with the fatal certainty and explosive holism of Dr. Mann. "This is not about my life, or Cooper's life; this is about all mankind. There is a moment—" As Dr. Mann (a man, too much of a man with that extra "n") endeavors to dispense with the remaining astronauts Cooper and Brand.

He gets rid of them in his speech about mankind, which is spoken as if that concept radically transcends its components, actually existing humans. And at that very moment, Mann's murderous holism proves indeed and ironically to be suicidally . . . explosive. Hubristically, Mann thinks he knows how to work the docking procedure, and the airlock blows open, destroying a huge part of the Endurance and sucking him into the vacuum of space. A fitting end to the Severed human, and a tragedy for the other lifeforms involved in this grand plan of survival (including those back on Earth, but also notably Cooper and Brand).

IT'S NOT POSSIBLE! NO—IT'S NECESSARY

At that very moment, Cooper simply switches on the engines of Lander 1 and proceeds to dock. He wants to live, working under almost impossible conditions. He is determined to save the world, which in this scene is just the humans and their little spinning ship trapped in another galaxy, but which of course means the larger endeavor it is part of, of the desperate attempt to restart Earth by leaving it en masse. One of power animal companions (they are not slaves or workers in contrast to him, they are more like a dutiful teenage son and playful, wise big brother), the dutiful robot CASE, weighs in: "It's not possible." "No—it's necessary," replies Cooper. CASE, who as a robot is made of automated human emotion and cognition, states something technically correct from the viewpoint of past data. "Cooper, there's no point in using our fuel to chase—" Cooper, speaking from the futurality that projects or tumbles over itself like a Slinky, a future moment he is trying to catch, like a fisherman casting a line, interrupts him: "Analyze the Endurance's spin." It's the most powerful moment in the film, the fulcrum around which everything turns.

Here's a new twist on the Kantian injunction. Not *you must because you can*, nor *you can because you must*. In terms of ecological politics that acknowledges the symbiotic real, it's *you must because you can't*.

This is not a case of cutting into a continuum to establish the Event. Nor is it a case of latching on to a concrescence in formation, the materialist alternative to the Event. Those two options are the poles of contemporary action theory. But Cooper's is a whole new form of action, in which the goal is to mesh with what is already occurring in such a way as to bring about change. To dock, to join, to reconnect the Severed parts, to allow oneself to be spun to the point of blacking out: the Endurance is rotating at 67 or 68 rpm, and Lander 1 has to match its spin to dock. Brand passes out and Cooper is left alone with CASE and TARS, who is working the docking mechanism. It is by no means clear that simply because TARS can presumably calibrate measurements far more accurately than Cooper, the attempt will succeed. Indeed, the power animal needs a bit of encouragement: "Come on TARS . . ." Cooper yells.

In a sense, TARS and CASE are the actually existing humans, allowing Cooper and Brand to subscend their parts and embody humankind as such. As I pointed out, an algorithm is automated human "style," in the very broad sense in which phenomenology means it. Style is one's overall appearance, not just the parts of which you're in control. As I was arguing earlier, style is the past: appearance is the past. Thus, an algorithm is a snapshot of a past series of modes of humankind, like a musical score. The robots represent an inevitably past human state.

This frees up Cooper and Brand to improvise, simply and with phenomenological sincerity to manifest humankind's unique creativity in its futural mode. To use a quantum-theoretical metaphor, the ground state of action is a *fascination*, namely appreciation that has been freed from the shackles of its anthropocentric scaling. Humankind in fascination mode shimmers like a sapphire in powerful sunlight. This isn't about "seeing" "something," mysteriously, because this capacity to be fascinated, to be palpated by the object—the other way around comes logically later—is the quantum of humankind's action.

It's not that there's humankind, and then it does something.

It's that the humankind-action is unfolding, manifesting. It's the way the humankind algorithm executes. The quantum of action has been alienated into a mode of being of a subject contemplating an object with some anthropocentrically scaled aesthetic appreciation mode. But what too-rigid action theories miss is that precisely within this very alienated mode, this subject's subjecting (how they execute themselves), its total phenomenological style, and so its objecthood as humankind in humankinding mode shines forth. And *humankinding mode is fascination.* Humankind sparkles with fascination. This mode contingently and finitely touches the symbiotic real, letting that real reach its fingers in.

The astronauts of *Interstellar* have named the black hole after that comical embodiment of the carnal carnivalesque, Gargantua: a fact that belies its terrifying qualities and points toward something to do with how to find the right solidarity affect. We shall see. Cooper does something very different than Dr. Mann. From within the black hole, Cooper watches his ship having broken up in the future, a horrific loop in which a weird relativistic effect causes his own ship to destroy itself. First Ranger 2 is enveloped in dust, then we see sparks that become ever more percussive and damaging, then an explosive glare as past and future come ever closer.

Cooper ejects from the spacecraft at the last possible moment, but even then it's not over. He finds himself falling into a tesseract, a multidimensional object within Gargantua built by Them, the uncanny others who are never named, who are helping the humans for some reason, one of whom seems to reach through metal into the Endurance to shake Brand's hand as they travel through the wormhole. At first despairing then rediscovering his mojo, Cooper succeeds in sending a message back in time to one single person, his own daughter. He is acting as an "author of the impossible," as both a character in and an author of his own story, reintegrated with his superpowers in a Feuerbachian way, which in the terms of this book, if we read *Interstellar* as an allegory, are parts of his pre-Severed self, the nonhumans that he subscends.[7] When we say *reintegrated*, we mean made a whole that is less than the sum of its parts; *returned to inconsistency*. The Severing was an attempt to make a heap consistent. So, environmentalist explosive holism in which all the parts are dissolved perfectly in the whole is not just a theistic retweet—it's definitely hostile to actual ecological politics!

In order to return to inconsistency, Cooper has to become at first the ultimate in *passivity*. Cooper has allowed himself to fall into something from which there can be no escape, at least not for three-dimensional beings. And now he is only repeating what has already occurred, pushing books off shelves and trying to communicate by pushing patterns of books in Morse code. But this is fully uncanny because it seems as if Cooper (maybe he's just lost his mind?) has forgotten that this has already happened. "Morse!" he yells as if he is improvising. We see here activity being haunted by passivity and vice versa, in a most uncanny, loop-like way. This is truly a new model for ethical and political action.

Whether it is acting or being acted on is radically undecidable, and I don't even know how to develop it much further within the confines of this book. But we have at least found the airport in which we are going to land the plane of human solidarity with nonhumans. This is not a compromise position *between* activity and passivity, but a whole new dimension that we might call wiggle room, rather like the temporal parts of Murph in the tesseract, lots of cubes like televisions or cubic crystal balls, with figures and actions jiggling around inside them. If there is a good word for the Buddhist notion of emptiness, it isn't a conceptual word, but an experiential one: *space*, which has nothing to do with absolute void, but rather with the relief of finding wiggle room, and the sense of humor we kindle when we say "wiggle." This new form of action has a necessarily *silly* component. It's interesting that the silly is the one affect we never ever think of as politically or ethically effective. Indeed, we might usually regard it as a nuisance or a waste. But silliness appears to be a pathway toward finding the wiggle room that joins us to nonhumans, including our pre-Severed actually existing symbiotic selves.

Cooper becomes his daughter's ghost, a spectral being haunting her past, in whom no one in their right Severed mind would believe. But Murph does believe. Cooper is both human and specter, uncannily just beside himself as he watches himself leaving Murph from behind the bookshelf. So, the 5-D Them, the super-beings, are not super in the sense of having transcended time and space or having achieved ultimate mastery; nor is being your own author a question of mastery, but a deeply confusing matter of self-haunting, as anyone who has had a paranormal experience will affirm. They are deeply ambiguous. Am I having something real or is this an illusion or a delusion? What type of illusion? What form of real? Am I in someone else's story or am I writing my own? Any good author will tell you that they do not in fact have authority, that they are involved in a hopeless chase of the wild goose of themselves through the necessarily temporal medium of narrative: "I am not wherever I am the plaything of my thought. I think of what I am where I do not think to think."[8] No, this is not transcendence and omnipotence and omnipresence. This is subscendence, allowing for solidarity with the nonhuman. What could be more nonhuman than a black hole?

In the tesseract, a 3-D representation of a 5-D reality, rejoining this nonhuman spectral realm is horribly disorienting and disturbing. As one becomes aware of more dimensions of oneself, that one is not in fact one nor dissolved into multiplicity, but haunted by spectral parts of oneself that are also not parts, that subscendently wiggle around all by themselves, one might go crazy. Cooper lets out a groan and despairing sobs, then screams and tears, as he watches himself ostensibly betraying his own daughter over and over again, the temporal parts of the scene subscendently wiggling around above and below and around him. He is trying for mastery. He is trying, as TARS puts it a moment later, "to change the past," which is often how we view dialectical action. He wishes he had never even tried to leave the poisoned Earth, to imagine something different, to fantasize. He breaks down in despair, resting his head against one of the bookcases floating in seemingly infinite 3-D confusion space.

Luckily his power animal TARS shows up, the friendly, witty, wise older brother in the uncanny form of a spectral radio voice somewhere above him, and snaps him out of it. Severed humankind is despairing. But within that very moment, *the despair is precisely a latching on to other beings*. Paranoia, the feeling of being haunted and watched, becomes a possibility condition for solidarity, which in a way is the subscendent affective parts of emotions such as empathy and sympathy.

Read that again: *paranoia is a possibility condition for solidarity*. Because I don't know whether or not you are or I am a person, I am paranoid, and as this ambiguity becomes ever more intense, I relate to you ever more intimately. It's going to be okay. As Cooper himself puts it, "We're the bridge." It's a bridge, not an ontological firewall. There is a thing called humankind, and we can access it, albeit in an anthropomorphic way, yet strangely in an anti-anthropocentric way. This is because humankind is a heap of things that aren't humankind. The theme of spatio-temporal dimensions gets at this. The 5-D beings can't see everything. They are limited, because unlike Cooper, "They can't find a specific point *in* time . . . they can't communicate." Seeing the heap of all the dimensions is not seeing the most real top level. A transfinite set is a group of numbers bisected by numbers from another dimension. There is no "bridge" between pi and the nearest rational number (the continuum hypothesis). Pi exists in another dimension.

Spectral humankind, in recovery from the Severing, is able to talk to Severed humankind, its very own self. And it does this from a futural mode that is truly a dimension that haunts and scoops out the present from the inside. Because the non-Severed symbiotic real is . . . well, real. It is ongoing.

Quanta are described by Richard Feynman as "tiny jiggling things," and it's quantum data that humans need. They need to find it in a black hole, which is a terribly serious-seeming, non-wiggly thing. But if gravity is like the other forces, it must be quantized. It must come in tiny jiggling blobs of energy—gravitons. Perhaps gravity is not grave after all. By definition, gravitons would not have time or space as we know them because gravitons *produce* space-time: that is the noise they make to beings such as us. The way gravitons relate might be much more like how we relate to our friends on Facebook, in clusters and bundles that are more or less dense.[9] The universe might have more space-time in certain parts, like lumpy porridge. Silly, jiggly inconsistency, subscendent lumps of space-time as such.

MISANTHROPOCENTRISM

Is anthropocentrism always a little self-hating? And does this self-hatred effectively express in a negative sense the trauma to us of excluding nonhumans?

Hope isn't a popular emotion on the left right now. But seeing through all utopian projects and sealing off all the exits is the net effect of cynical reason, which has become very attractive among leftist intellectuals. If we were going to boil the attitude of cynical reason down to one sentence, it would be this: *I am smarter than you because I can see through you.* She is a totally deluded fool, you are an atrocious hypocrite, but I am completely free of illusion. We could remember Lacan at this point: "*les non-dupes errent*" means that ideology has no more powerful a grip than when you think you are free of it. Ecological reality does not allow us the luxury of fantasizing that we can achieve escape velocity from our phenomenological style. The sentence "All sentences are ideological," is a distillation of a certain Althusserian version of cynical reason. But if all sentences are ideological, then so must this sentence be, and we have an infinite regress. The Left seems to have busied itself with the impossible task of finding the ultimate policeman to arrest all the other policemen and all the other characters in the Monty Python "Argument Clinic" sketch.[10]

There is something very claustrophobic about the impossibility of cynical reason. We find ourselves hemmed in, tied down, worrying about our place in the dirt as Cooper puts it, trapped. Ecological awareness *is* claustrophobic. You find yourself surrounded, permeated, composed of not-you beings. And you are phenomenologically glued to Earth. Say we do travel to another planet. We will need to recreate a terrestrial biosphere, possibly from scratch—we will have the same problem as we have down here on Earth, only magnified.

Ecoclaustrophobia means that we can be *more cynical than cynical reason*. Think about another sentence: *All tactics are hypocritical.* This must mean that the sentence is also hypocritical. Something is always missing from the ethical and political ecological jigsaw, which means that there can be no top-level political form to rule them all. How to exit from a trap in which expected exit strategies are just different ways of reinforcing it? The exit appears to be "inside" trap space, or as *Interstellar* might put it, in another dimension that's right here, but inaccessible for now to us 3-D beings.

The logic of the neighbor or of the stranger is the logic of the symbiotic real, not the logic of friend and enemy. Sovereignty and exception and decision are not capable of operating with the symbiotic real in mind, because they are based on a logic of exclusion. Stranger-logic means that the whole that is the biosphere is subscendent: it is tattered and jagged, it has pieces missing, it's less than the sum of its parts. It might then be the case that there can be no totality to rule them all, and that if this is only what communism means, we cannot think communism without metaphysical universalisms concerning the human. If, however, it is possible to imagine a host of communisms then we will be able to include nonhumans in communist thought. Interdependence (the basic fact of ecology) means that one lifeform is always excluded from a group: caring for rabbits means not caring for rabbit predators. Communisms can only be contingent, fragile and playful. Trying to resurrect the Axial Age god one more time—once more with feeling!—is the problem about which Feuerbach is so eloquent.

Fragile, "anarchist" (pejorative term) communisms that are necessary if we are to include nonhumans requires thought that engages with more unlikely sources: not only Kropotkin, but also Stirner. At a certain level, being-with is not just "individuals" cooperating but a weird loop in which I do not quite coincide with myself: the first form of coexistence is denigrated as narcissism. In some strong sense, I am not the same as "my" experience. Experience as such is also something like a nonhuman being.

Stirner as well as Kropotkin? Of course. Despite its conscious claims to maximum efficiency, we see the same paradox (the goal is happiness, the result is misery) exemplified in the current state of Mesopotamia, neoliberal capitalism. Neoliberal bureaucracy, the totally inefficient self-scrutiny and setting of "outcomes" in the name of "excellence" and "effectiveness," utterly similar to Stalinist or Maoist control tactics, and the bad faith with which these exercises are administered and carried out by all participants, is surely just the latest incarnation of the Axial Age patriarchal god with his arbitrary, superego-driven, "evil," impossible and incomprehensible commands.

Self-displacement is *the quintessential gesture of anthropocentrism*, as we can see in the rhetoric of the Singularity-obsessed in Silicon Valley, waiting for that glorious day when artificial intelligence will have developed beyond the human. This will, they like to say, enable humans to unleash the full capacity of their compassion through billions of tiny, powerful prosthetic computational devices. They won't unleash the compassion right now; that would make them look foolish. Or they will freeze themselves to await a brighter future where their plans and minds will have been respected for the genius that they embody. Such wishes are clearly ecologically destructive in themselves (think how much energy cryogenic suspension would take, let alone how many minerals tiny computers the size of red blood cells would require). The human is precisely the force that displays itself as transhuman.

The radical—what? "Individualism" is the wrong word—of Stirner provides a powerful corrective. "The State Socialists love to assert that at present we live in the age of individualism; the truth, however, is that individuality was never valued at so low a rate as today": what Baginski means is that there is no way to be unique, that individualism is a mode of traumatized survival.[11] Then we need to apply this thought to humankind as such, which Stirner begins: "Mankind looks only at itself, mankind will promote the interests of mankind only, mankind is its own cause."[12] Stirner shows a pathway toward integrating the severed capacities of humankind. Such a reintegration can only ultimately point to a reintegration of the severed nonhuman, by logical extension. Stirner implies it by resisting the temptation to fill out the notion of selfhood with a positive content: "I am the creative nothing, the nothing out of which I myself as creator create everything."[13] It might seem paradoxical that Stirner can be used to reboot the symbiotic real within social, psychic and thought space. Consider, however, his riposte to Feuerbach, which provides an important modification for our purposes:

> Let us, in brief, set Feuerbach's theological view and our contradiction over against each other! "The essence of man is man's supreme being; now by religion, to be sure, the supreme being is called God and regarded as an objective essence, but in truth it is only man's own essence; and therefore the turning point of the world's history is that henceforth no longer God, but man, is to appear to man as God."
>
> To this we reply: The supreme being is indeed the essence of man, but, just because it is his essence and not he himself, it remains quite immaterial whether we see it outside him and view it as "God," or find it in him and call it "Essence of Man" or "Man." I am neither God nor Man, neither the supreme essence nor my essence, and therefore it is all one in the main whether I think of the essence as in me or outside me.[14]

If this is individualism, then it's a haunted, subscendent individualism, shadowy and flickering: X-individualism. I do not coincide with my "essence," with humankind. Otherwise we are stuck with the explosively holist theistic alternative: "Every higher essence, e.g. truth, mankind, etc., is an essence *over* us."[15]

We don't need to reject the idea of thinking at a magnitude sufficient to think species. Instead, we need to reject the theistic version that I am forced to visualize by the PR of large corporations. In rejecting this, we should not skip over the idea of species altogether and hide in our correlationist bunker of human architects, bees not allowed. Realizing that we are parts of humankind is the first step toward a communism that could and must include nonhumans.

ADORNO'S DINOS

Adorno's prose microwaves things like plastic dinosaurs. But he kept them on his desk at Columbia University. His wife called him Teodont, a mashup of *Theodor* and a dinosaur tooth (the *-dont* suffix).

Plastic dinosaurs are nonhumans, and kitsch nonhumans at that: kitsch, despite his official view, which was that kitsch was fascist. Toy nonhumans are thus ironically in accord with his view that true progress looks like regression.[16] How can someone hold both views at the same time? The unofficial, cute-dinosaur-loving Adorno seems at odds, poor man, with the official Schoenberg-lionizing one. Oddly, this is indeed thought's encounter with non-identity, which is as I've mentioned before how Adorno describes the dialectic. Literally: the empirical, phenomenological Adorno is a cute little Teodont with plastic dinosaurs—and the spectral Hegelian thought realm he inhabits encounters it . . . and spurns it as fascist or as commodity fetishist.

Along with never mentioning the dinosaurs, Adorno was none too pleased with spiritualism, and like Engels ("Natural Science in the Spirit World") thought to write against it.[17] His 1940s essay against the occult doesn't mince words:

> The occultist draws the ultimate conclusion from the fetish-character of commodities: menacingly objectified labour assails him on all sides from demonically grinning objects. What has been forgotten in

a world congealed into products, the fact that it has been produced by men, is split off and misremembered as a being-in-itself added to that of the objects and equivalent to them. Because objects have frozen in the cold light of reason, lost their illusory animation, the social quality that now animates them is given an independent existence both natural and supernatural, a thing among things.[18]

It is almost as if he is being animated by the exact type of spectral being that he is afraid of and angry about—for what could be more like that than the Geist of Hegel, whose mode Adorno desperately tries to exorcise, while remaining within it? His line about the encounter with non-identity is from his most profound wrestle with Hegel.

What Adorno is describing isn't commodity fetishism at all. Commodity fetishism isn't a cognitive state of any kind (belief, attitude, feeling, thought). That's what is fetishistic about it: the fact that it's not an optional extra. Commodity fetishism *is* an "agency of the object," that is to say, it has nothing to do with the things we call people (humans, give or take), despite how some Marxists seem to think that caring about fridges and golf balls means you are an evil capitalist commodity fetishist. Commodity fetishism is how the *commodity itself* appears to compute value in its spiriting away of abstract surplus labor time. Commodity fetishism doesn't depend on not knowing the labor theory of value, and the labor theory of value is already part of capitalist value theory. It would be truly magical if simply remembering the labor theory of value cured the world of capitalism. That sounds New Age Hegelian itself: "If we all think really hard, maybe the rain will stop," as the MC at Woodstock put it. And the demonically grinning objects— of course they aren't seductively smiling—appear to be out of some Hegelian cartoon of "prehistorical" Africa. No one forgets that products are made by humans.

And even if they did, that forgetting would be irrelevant to commodity fetishism, which proceeds in the nonhuman realm, outside of human "subjectivity," despite our thoughts and feelings and intentions. Here lies the real source of Adorno's panic against the idea of panic that "undoes the gains of enlightenment and establishes, in the wake of the death of God, a 'second mythology.'"[19]

It's precisely the magical power of surplus labor time, "the goose that laid the golden eggs" (*Capital*, vol. 1), that drives the transmutation of M into M′ in Marx's famous formula for capitalism, M–C–M′.[20] Surplus labor time is a *specter*. What Marx is saying in that paragraph on the commodity fetish is that the realm of capitalism is *more* supernatural than the realm of telekinetically moving tables, not *less*. Commodity fetishism isn't a false belief. It's a distorted actuality. Furthermore, it precisely has to do with *not* caring about commodities as things or objects or what have you. Commodity fetishism doesn't care whether the thing in question is a golf ball or a nuclear warhead. Caring about things that are not human doesn't make you a commodity fetishist; *not caring about them* is exactly what commodity fetishism is all about. A golf ball and a nuclear warhead become value computers, equally blank screens in a virtual stock exchange.

He is notoriously hyper-intelligent—so what possessed Adorno to forget all this? Precisely—what possessed him? It is as if Adorno is *possessed* by a style that is distinctly Hegelian in tone. He can't seem to help himself. The specter of Geist floats uncannily behind the shoulder of phenomenal Adorno, Teodont with his plastic dinosaurs. The fact that Adorno stutters over the most basic Marxist theory at this precise moment is deeply significant. Teodont would have made a better Marxist!

But that would mean the Left would need to embrace the idea that wanting to revolutionize society is about wanting to be comfy. As the philosopher himself says, the image of peace, "*rien faire comme une bête*," just floating and looking at the sky, is a powerful image of utopia.[21] "Nothing to do, like a wild animal"; this nothing-to-do is precisely species-being, the wild animal quality of humankind that leaks out everywhere like the silk emerging from the silkworm, Marx's image (if you recall) for how Milton wrote his masterpiece. Nothing to do—*doing* here is post-Severing anthropocentric action, becoming ever more frantic. Plastic dinosaurs just sit there.

The frenzied decisionism of correlationist action theory has led to an overemphasis on the death drive: "Standing in the place of the death drive," as Lacan puts it, maniacal blind machinating, as opposed to the pleasure orientation we are exploring here. Survival is all about the overkill of the death drive. In *Interstellar*, Dr. Mann says of Professor Brand, who has secretly never believed in getting humans off the planet, "He was prepared to destroy his own humanity in order to save the species. He made an incredible sacrifice," without a shred of irony. Comfy Marxism is about moving toward the other pole of death, absolute non-existence, but not all the way: remaining in that quivering place between the two types of death, the quivering we call life and the quivering we call beauty, a signal of death indeed, without the actuality of death.

To become a dreaded object—how Adorno's prose bemoans that awful fate! Objects don't even really exist for the Hegelian, so this is truly a fate worse than death, akin to the fate called *being a woman*, according to that Hegelian, Lacan. One would become a blank screen, without even extensional properties of one's own. The logic goes like this: hypnotized by capitalism, the spiritualist's sin is flat ontology, spirit has become "a thing among things." If the (human) spirit is the one Decider that gets to make things real, the results sound awful. Everything becomes a meaningless blank because in Hegel's solution to Kant, the thing is a blank screen for desire projection purposes, an artifact of spirit as such: the transcendental gap between thing and phenomenon is happening within the (human) subject.

But the realm of the "object" (the nonhuman in its most basic guise) is precisely the realm in which commodity fetishism is happening. And this is precisely what makes it *more* supernatural than thinking that tables can dance when influenced by some spiritual force. Capitalism is illusion squared, appearing deceptively as disillusion—which is a pretty accurate paraphrase of a large section of the *Communist Manifesto*. Which in turn means that Adorno's haunted prose, possessed by the Geist of Hegel, enacts on one level what it utterly disavows on another!

Adorno was a Freudian Marxist of sorts. For Freud, the uncanny isn't about the spectral: it's the juicing of the modern subject on the weirdness of its physical grounding in the body, specifically the vagina out of which it was born. Knowing coexisting with disavowal. To cross over to spectral experience is to short-circuit the frisson of the uncanny. But, as I've argued, this kind of uncanniness has a very limited shelf life. What an effort to preserve it! Perhaps this is the deep reason for its perpetual reiteration—the fact that it is circling around a disavowed "animism" or as Adorno puts it, tellingly, "*animal*ism" (my emphasis), that ends up, even on this view, being the only real show in town. The uncanny is how it looks when you half shut your eyes to it. What is sinful about acknowledging the spectral is that it amplifies this teetering, fragile aesthetic experience until it loses its anthropocentric scaling.

And what is this experience other than a feeling of solidarity with nonhuman beings? And what is *that*, in turn, if not an acknowledgment of the symbiotic real? The stillness Adorno evokes is more profound than the radically passive stasis of a Bartleby and his "I would prefer not to." In that case, we have the ethical equivalent of an inert, bland substance without qualities. But reality isn't like that. It sparkles. Bartleby is the object of sadism because he typifies precisely the sadistic ideal object, an inert bland substance that simply resists. Bartleby is to ethics as vanilla atoms (extensional lumps) are to ontology. The narrator finally exclaims, "Ah Bartleby! Ah humanity!" at the end of "Bartleby, the Scrivener."[22] By now we can feel the resonance of that term Humanity: Bartleby is a vanilla substance component of an explosively holist vanilla substance.

What we want is not the ethical atomism of total refusal, but a quantum theory where acting and being-acted-on aren't the binary that they are in theistic action theories. Yes, the Levinasian intuition that there's something wrong with action theory is correct. But the Levinasian solution is part of the problem.

Action isn't different from passion. Action is made of little quantized dots of passion. The quantum of action looks like passivity because it's receptivity, not because it's inertia. It isn't just negation; it is a quivering, "living" (compromised word) vibration, an undead spectral life common to both lifeforms and to non-life. Here is Adorno again: "'Being, nothing else, without any further definition and fulfillment' . . . None of the abstract concepts comes closer to fulfilled utopia than that of eternal peace."[23] His image is of an exhausted consciousness, staring blankly—the kind of gesture one finds in Buddhist meditation instruction, in which the meditator is enjoined not to make an effort but to allow experiences to take place simply, without blocking them. Rather than cryogenic stasis or the death drive of inorganic quiescence, the Buddhaphobic image of total passivity, the stillness is the quantum of action, of species-being: species-being, nothing else.

MUTUAL AID

If solidarity is the noise that the symbiotic real makes, we could imagine that mutual aid is just a paraphrase of the term symbiotic. Mutual aid is the slogan of the anarchist Peter Kropotkin. We need to haunt Marxism with another specter: the specter of anarchism. Anarchism split from socialism after the First International, in 1872. But what if Marxism only thrives when it is ghosted by its spectral halo, anarchism?

This is strikingly evident when it comes to thinking human–nonhuman relations because in order to do that we need first to think nonhuman–nonhuman relations. We need to deconstruct the selfishness–altruism binary that is a violent artifact of agrilogistic functioning and its utilitarian subroutine. Altruism is how utilitarianism imagines doing things or feeling things for other people. Even if we got over the self-concept/no-self-concept binary, and the act/behave binary, we would be left wondering what on earth kindness consists of, and what on earth we can do to promulgate it.

The very word "altruism" is a self-defeating setup, along the lines of the Schopenhauerian prejudice about Buddhism: how can you desire to get rid of your desire? When it comes to altruism, how can *you*, a *self*, allow yourself to be *un-selfish*?

Enter Prince Kropotkin, the geographer of St. Petersburg.

It is becoming less and less possible to maintain that at least mammals and even birds don't feel emotion. Chimps and bonobos save their young from drowning, even though they can't swim. Rats will rescue fellow rats from cages and give them food first (empathy and compassion, and an "altruistic" act).[24] This kind of phenomenon is surely not altruism, self-abnegation for the sake of the group—isn't that another example of explosive holism? It's much more like what Kropotkin calls "mutual aid." Kropotkin's work is peppered with examples too numerous to mention, and this kind of approach, too, is becoming more and more prevalent in current ethological and ecological research. Kropotkin's first appendix is on swarms, and the second one is on ants. He talks about how beetles and ants bury their dead. He talks about ants caring for one another: there is "no quarrel" over who gets to lay their eggs in an animal carcass.

We will need to modify him, though, for our purposes. Kropotkin evokes the Great Chain of Being, which is an unnecessary and teleological concept that has less than nothing to do with evolution theory per se.[25] Kropotkin regards some animals as "higher" than others; some are more "noble" because they are more "complex." None of this is particularly Darwinian. The randomness and nonhierarchy of Darwinian theory needs to be preserved, without the bug, the "survival of the fittest" canard that he was forced to put in by nervous social Darwinists—the concepts underpinning what we now call "social Darwinism" having arisen in fact *before* Darwin actually published *The Origin of Species*. The myths of the predatory law of the jungle and the alpha male (a now debunked view of how wolves organize themselves) are Feuerbachian displacements of human ideological capacities onto nonhumans, otherwise known as naturalization.[26]

What Kropotkin helps us to think through, however, are the issues around altruism, anthropomorphism and anthropocentrism, because the last two need to be disambiguated in such a way that we can rewrite "altruism" to mean something that could actually work.

This is how Kropotkin commences that task. He begins notably by showing that specific acts of kindness are shadowed by a penumbra that readers of this book should by now come to see immediately as our good old friend, the spectral:

> It is not love to my neighbour—whom I often do not know at all— which induces me to seize a pail of water and to rush towards his house when I see it on fire; it is a far wider, even though more vague feeling or instinct of human solidarity and sociability which moves me. So it is also with animals. It is not love, and not even sympathy (understood in its proper sense) which induces a herd of ruminants or of horses to form a ring in order to resist an array of wolves.[27]

Brilliantly, Kropotkin takes the burden off the individual lifeform while allowing species to be thought as groups and collectives. We don't have to look for "love" or "even sympathy." What we are after is much more basic: solidarity. The blending of human with nonhuman here is very significant, as is the use of the Christian discourse of "love thy neighbor." Nonhumans are being thought as neighbors, a concept far more intense than thinking them as "companion species" or as beings under our stewardship.[28] Indeed, Kropotkin goes so far as to say that our own human tendency to solidarity is *inherited* from nonhumans:

> I have tried to indicate in brief the immense importance which the mutual-support instincts, inherited by mankind from its extremely long evolution, play even now in our modern society, which is supposed to rest upon the principle: "every one for himself, and the State for all," but which it never has succeeded, nor will succeed in realizing.

Kropotkin begins to describe swarms as solidarity behavior. The response on social media regarding Cecil the lion is well described as swarm behavior. Kropotkin describes the fate of those gulls who don't participate in their solidarity; robbers of nests are kept in check.[29] Is it truly anthropomorphism to talk about emotion and solidarity? The idea that it is anthromorphic to do so seems to beg the question. Whether or not the tactic is anthropomorphic, the actual enemy is not anthropomorphism, it is *anthropocentrism*, an entirely different beast that can express itself *either* by humanizing the nonhuman or indeed by totally dehumanizing it.

Paleolithic humans are only different in degree from contemporary ones insofar as Paleolithic ones are less aware of the indirect consequences of their actions. So, given all this loved-upness, why do humans have any tendency to undermine mutual aid at all? Unions keep reconstituting themselves even when suppressed. The violence of neoliberalism is necessary to break through mutual aid to the extent that mutual aid is intrinsic to humankind. Kropotkin is not sentimentalizing working-class people when he writes, "For every one who has any idea of the life of the labouring classes it is evident that without mutual aid being practised among them on a large scale they never could pull through all their difficulties."[30] What is meant is that cooperation is the zero-degree, cheapest coexistence mode, something you rely on when all else fails. Mutual aid is not teleological. Symbiosis cannot be thought teleologically.

Soviet Marxism was not averse to symbiosis: two notable thinkers in this regard were Konstantin Mereschkowski and Andrei Famitsyn.[31] The Soviets went so far as to presuppose endosymbiosis. But this raised the problem of Lysenkoism, which amounts to a suspension of belief in evolution theory. This is an artifact of the anthropocentric, Hegelian bug in Marxism. Engels had produced his own more ostensibly "dialectical" account of evolution soon after Darwin, adding back the teleology that Darwin had been so careful to remove, for which Marx admired Darwin greatly.[32] In *Dialectics of Nature*, Engels makes an open-ended case for labor as the driver of human evolution, starting with some interesting thoughts about the dexterity of the hand. But eventually he lapses into the teleological version of species-being: "The animal merely *uses* its environment, and brings about changes in it simply by its presence; man by his changes makes it serve his ends, *masters* it. This is the final, essential distinction between man and other animals."[33]

Kropotkin, on the other hand, cheapens (in a good way) the concept of labor into the concept of play, and this is more promising if we want to resist teleology. Even hares appear to play.[34] Kropotkin takes play to be deeper than parenting. Solidarity is a possibility condition for play. Because entities are structurally incomplete, they require solidarity to play themselves out. If play is a deeper category than reified notions of work or labor, then what does that say about how we act? What is political action, taking humankind into consideration? A communism that allows for nonhuman beings requires nothing less than a strongly de-anthropocentrized rewriting of action theory. What would that look like?

ROCKING: A NEW THEORY OF ACTION

Political action theory tends to be deeply anthropocentric. This depends on current concepts of event. There are two main types of event concepts: the cutting-into-a-continuum type, and the continuum type. The latter is the new Whiteheadian kid on the philosophical block. The former is the Badiou-style theory of the Event, or indeed the Deleuzian theory of desiring machines, or the structuralist theory of language.

The problem is, there is no such thing as this continuum! Instead, there are actually existing lifeforms.

At the Event pole of action theory, acting has been metaphysically construed as cutting by some privileged Decider. The discourse of the Event is a displacement of human supernatural powers into a quasi-divine domain, where a godlike human (but who appointed them to this role?) gets to decide what happens and when in a drastic way—gets to decide how happening at all will appear. Event theory is caught in misanthropocentric apocalypticism. Revolutions and Big Bangs are fetishized as theistic miracles, something coming from nothing, and in the case of revolution, it's just the same old patriarchal story about some transcendental, dictatorial Decider decreeing that things get underway, cutting into a continuum. Let there be light. When you add quantum equations to those based on general relativity that explain the Big Bang, you find that there have been lots of medium-sized bangs.[35] Maybe we should start normalizing revolution for quivering vibrating stillness. Maybe then we could have many more of them. Maybe they wouldn't be so scary and difficult to think about, then, because the basic energy of revolution is just the basic energy of non-theistic miracle, of the illusion-like magical display that is the fuel of causality. Normalizing revolution would mean that there isn't one violent Big Bang of the Event, but lots of medium-sized bangs where violence is distributed throughout the symbiotic real, heavily diluted. It's the attempt to avoid violence altogether, like the attempt to "live" in the sense of "survive," that generates the worst kinds of violence.

How do we come back down to Earth? By a spectral pathway. We need to reintroduce what is called *passivity* into our theory of action. Not the radical passivity of the Levinasians, but a spectral passivity that must haunt what is called activity as a condition of its possibility.

Things can happen not because of the count-as-one (a component of Event theory) but because of the subscedence-into-many. Like thousands of baby spiders bursting out of an egg sac, things themselves contain the wiggle room that allows for stuff to happen. Some philosophers seem hell bent on preventing things from happening. They suffer from a peculiar philosophical disorder called *kinephobia*, or fear of movement. Or they want things to happen by being Decided on by some correlator. Or they want things to happen through the agency of some mysterious force external to things (ultimately, this will involve a prime mover of some kind, a switch flipper, and a mechanistic view of reality).

For Hegel, the correlator (Spirit) contains its own Slinky-like quality of being able to flop over itself. This is a promising idea if we drop the anthropocentrism and dial down (but not eliminate) the correlationism. Micro-Hegel is generally awesome: Hegel subscends Hegel that way. Macro-Hegel is what justifies invading Africa and China. In the world of macro-Hegel, the Slinky is implausibly capable of going *upstairs*. In fact, it can only go upstairs. The problem is repeated at another level when it comes to a certain phase of the phenomenology of spirit. Micro-Hegel's description of the beautiful soul is just a wonderful explication of many things that afflict our world, in particular in the realm of environmentalism. But the irony is that macro-Hegel is a beautiful soul activation device. The smug powerlessness of cynical reason and its critique mode is strong evidence of this.

This is of course the good old idea of dialectical movement, the movement that is the dialectic. And so it seems beyond important that we are now going to look at the Marxist notion of that dialectic and see what happens when we think it through the concept of subscendence. Marx claims to have fixed the bug in Hegel by flipping him upside down. The dialectic is now not internal to Spirit (whatever that is) but to what Marx calls the material level, which is to say (for him) the level of (human) economic relations. Everything else gets to be mechanically pushed by everything else (prime mover alert!), but that's more just shuffling, not movement as such.

Houston, we have a problem.

So, we can fix the problem. Imagine a Slinky that slunk without its rings being pulled down a convenient step. Visualize that strange, flopping, falling motion. We can only fix our problem by allowing things to move all by themselves, and making "move" mean something quite robust, rather than simply "be mechanically shuffled around."

Which, in turn, means that we need to let tables dance. Houston, we have another problem.

Actually, we need to let tables rock.

Which kind of problem do we want? As amazing and difficult to swallow as it seems, we need the second kind of problem: the world in which tables can dance. This would be the world in which Slinkies can wriggle around by themselves, *wriggle* being part of the etymological resonance of *rocking*.

I am going to define rocking as *spectral action*, namely an action that subscends hardcore correlationism and hardcore materialism and includes the spectral, the spectral nonhuman. Quantum events are notoriously difficult to pin down; they are profoundly ambiguous and appear to have no causal mechanism "behind" them. Pretty much all such "loopholes" (the term used in the scientific literature) have been ruled out in research on the spooky phenomenon of nonlocality, where a particle entangled with another particle polarizes in a complementary way *simultaneously*—radically violating Einstein's speed limit, the speed of light, yet also violating the mechanical materialism on which the other going theory of action, the non-Hegelian materialist one, depends.

Spectral action will look spooky, or like nothing at all, or impossible, or magical, depending on what kind of a person you are. The revolution will not be televised, but that's not all: it won't be possible to point to it in any way whatsoever, because quantum action can't be located in one region of space-time, nor can it be reduced to smaller, easier-to-identify bits. There are no atoms of quantum action. One New Age interpretation of quantum theory is simply correlationism in an off-the-shelf form. I wonder whether it is unconsciously also a way to *contain* what is most interesting about quantum theory—and more disturbingly, to reassert the Severed human obsession with being the Decider.

Our going theories of action are hamstrung by a distortion within correlationism itself, a distortion that is the footprint of nonhuman beings, present in their absence as specters. This new theory of action is hamstrung from the start by the rigid metaphysical distinction Western philosophy has tended to draw between the local and the global, which it imagines as the universal. This universality is in turn imagined in an explosively holist way, as a whole that is greater than the sum of its parts, and this image also hampers the development of a new theory of action. A new theory of action would alter how we think violence, which would be equivalent to a deep shift in notions of solidarity. Violence, in the new theory of action, would belong not to the greater explosive whole but to the fragile contingency (of whatever size). There would be a host of micro-violences (even though they might be ever so large), rather than a pantheon of macro-violences. Ecological awareness means that in any political grouping something is necessarily excluded—there is a fundamental fragility and inconsistency about any set of political beings. This necessary exclusion is the locus of violence, such that solidarity is always in the structural position of wishing it could encompass more, encompass everything. But this wish is just exactly the feeling of compassion, in its most default, least hyped-up state, a passion-to-coexist, a striving-to-be-with.

I describe as *rocking* the inner dynamic of action based on a readily available solidarity that includes nonhuman beings. What does the verb "to rock" usually mean?

A ship moving in intense waters is rocking and rolling. Humans having sex rock and roll. Rock and roll is a musical form involving driving drums, swiveling hips, riffing guitars. The early modern German "*rocken*," a rare term for wiggling the butt. To sway gently. The Swedish "*rucka*," to move to and fro.³⁶ Rocking gathers a whole set of resonances to do with moving in place, oscillation, moving while standing still. Dancing, what a Russian formalist called movement that is felt. But dancing is also movement that isn't going anywhere.³⁷ It keeps snapping back to its starting position.

If we pay attention, we can glimpse something very strange in these resonances: a whole new theory of action. This theory of action has to do with a highly necessary queering of the theistic categories of *active* versus *passive*, categories that are deeply caught in the way we think sexualities and the cultures and politics of those sexualities. These are categories that, going further, violently interfere with the way humans have treated nonhumans in social, psychic and philosophical space. Only consider how sexuality and in particular queerness in rock music has been expressed and policed, since its inception, to begin to intuit how urgent and quiveringly sensitive this issue is. It is high time to retire the concepts *active* and *passive* as we commonly think them, and time to start rocking.

Let us punningly consider geological rocks for a moment. We assume that what rocks do is stand perfectly still. Rocks are supposed to be part of Nature, the background to our foreground, the rugged parts of it that we can latch onto with our moving feet and hands if we are so inclined. The reassuringly static reserve of geo-stuff waits to be cut and exploded and melted and smelted and turned into pleasant slabs of kitchen countertop.[38]

We expect rocks to play their part, which is to say, be totally passive. We're the top, they're the bottom and we expect them to stay that way. When they play at being the top, humans call it an earthquake and find it highly unpleasant. Or, consider a rock falling on one's car: there are road hazard signs showing how it happens, but we never read those signs as if the rocks somehow jump off the cliff and hurtle down toward us. We are hampered even from beginning to ascribe intention to rocks, the issue that lurks in the background of the notion of agency.

We are wary of letting rocks do things because we are wary of letting agency be about doing things. We talk about distributed agency, or emergent agency, as a way to signal our discomfort, but this is the merest hint. Calling agency "distributed" means that one doesn't really need to claim that this rock is acting. It is part of a network of actants, instead, acting insofar as it has effects on other things. It would be indecorous to pin the acting down to any one part of the network. There is an unspoken prohibition on appearing a philistine in these matters; to acknowledge distribution is an aesthetic preference in an age of anxiety about authority.

Does this not also sound like theism, however? *Active* and *passive* have to do with souls in bodies, namely with the Neoplatonic

Christianity that thought insists, even now, on retweeting, often unconsciously—which is to bring up the notion of passivity, which is to invite attack. One of the principal rules of polite speech is never to mention the unconscious in public, because it suggests that part of the way we talk and act is unintended, passive in some sense. But ecological awareness is about acknowledging what one avant-garde musician calls *un-intention*.[39] In an insightful passage in *Dialectics of Nature*, Engels connects ecological awareness with the erasure of binaries that he traces to Christianity:

> The people who, in Mesopotamia, Greece, Asia Minor and elsewhere, destroyed the forests to obtain cultivable land, never dreamed that by removing along with the forests the collecting centers and reservoirs of moisture they were laying the basis for the present forlorn state of those countries . . . we are more than ever in a position to realise, and hence to control . . . the more remote natural consequences of at least our day-to-day production activities. But the more this progresses the more will men not only feel but also know their oneness with nature, and the more impossible will become the senseless and unnatural idea of a contrast between mind and matter, man and nature, soul and body, such as arose after the decline of classical antiquity in Europe and obtained its highest elaboration in Christianity.[40]

Does the gratifying illusion of activity versus passivity not sound a little like good old, or rather bad old, omnipresent omniscience? And does that not begin also to hint at that third excellent part of the Neoplatonic recipe, omnipotence? Potency, everywhere, flat potency, flat presence, flat knowing. This establishes the idea that not all access modes are equal, and that, in particular, knowing is the top access mode, and indeed the access mode for tops, otherwise known as human beings, mostly white Western ones with the right kind of sexuality. The prospect of liberating chimpanzees from zoos begins to sound remoter than ever. We assume we will first have to ascertain how to allow them to be white Western patriarchal heterosexual human males first.

Revolution begins to look as if it isn't in the cards either, since we can't even get a chimp out of a zoo. The distributed agency concept is simply an *ambient* version of the theistic patriarchal concept, like the original ambient music that Brian Eno heard because his record player was broken and only played things very quietly.[41] Super-low-volume patriarchy that won't disturb the neighbors: the institutions that make scholarly life slightly less unbearable by making it slightly more permanent.

Consider the puzzling phrase "Do what you feel." Notice that the phrase is not "Do whatever you feel like doing." It would be less difficult to understand that one. Is it that one is supposed to be feeling something, and then somehow performing this feeling to another? And if so, what is the status of the "and then"—is it a chronological "then" or a "logical" then? Is doing simultaneous with feeling, but feeling is the condition of possibility for this doing? It all seems uncertain and ambiguous. For instance, is it that by a certain doing we get to feel something? The syntax suggests this logic: another way to read the injunction is "What you feel is what you are doing." Whatever you do, there you are, feeling that. In this case, doing is logically prior to feeling, although in this case, also, it is far from obvious that chronologically you do, then you feel.

This phrase is sung over and over again in one of my favorite dance tunes, "Do What You Feel" by Joey Negro.[42] On examination this techno musician's output suggests that he struggled with this phrase too, and found it very compelling yet was never entirely sure exactly how to say it—or indeed, how to *do it*. There are several prototypes of this song, which became a hit on the rave scene about 1991.

There are more lyrics in some versions of the tune, but in those most popular at the time, there is only this one and one more, "Don't stop the body rock." As a matter of fact, one version does include the word "higher," which makes things much worse. You're supposed to be doing what you're feeling, only higher and higher—do it higher, or feel it higher. Or, without beating about the bush too much, you feel really high and you start lashing out blissfully. Or—it just got confusing again—you're describing the phenomenology of doing what you're feeling. Philosophers should never be allowed on the dance floor. Or maybe they should *only* be allowed on dance floors, because that's where their intellect might become confused enough to say something of significance.

Rocking one's body, or indeed someone else's, or enjoying the sensation of two or more people rocking, as in the Michael Jackson song "Rock with You," is obviously a favorite techno theme. "Meltdown" by Quartz—imagine the temperature at which quartz would start melting—contains the simple, demurely sung instruction "Rock your body."[43] And Derrick May's wonderful remix of Reese's "Rock to the Beat" turns that phrase into something like a lullaby, as the singer intones "Rock" with a long, expanded and melodically rising—then floating, then falling—lilt.[44] It sounds so gentle, slightly spooky, dark and even slightly sinister, evoking the way in which the techno drug of choice doesn't quite live up to its name, if by that name we expect happiness. MDMA or ecstasy seems to enhance awareness of what some Asian medical and spiritual systems call the subtle body, which is not exactly physical in a crude (as those systems say, "gross") sense, but not exactly mental either. The drug appears to operate "between" these categories, although *between* is also the wrong word, because the sensation of subtle body awareness is not unlike becoming aware of an alien entity, yet an alien that is more intimate than one's concept of oneself or one's sense of physical embodiment, aptly named, with its associations with that dreaded notion of property and propriety, *proprioception*. It somewhat resembles what Jack Halberstam says about the queer qualities of certain horror modes, in which something appears encrypted, hidden, or entombed within oneself, always already having penetrated oneself before one even became oneself.[45] It resembles what Freud pathologizes as introjection, and which Mária Török recuperates by imagining the ways the human psyche contains encrypted, entombed ghost beings.[46] The umbrella ontological term under which these psychic entities sit is the spectrality that forms a basic feature of the things we slightly wrongly call lifeforms, how hovering around—or is it within? or is it outside of?—an entity is a certain spectral version of itself, like the dæmons in Philip Pullman's *His Dark Materials* series. Here we encounter a healthy confusion of inside and outside, those categories that mark, for Derrida, the conditions for a metaphysics of presence.[47] Once thought has established an inside–outside distinction, the metaphysics of presence are just around the corner. People who report kundalini awareness, for example—and this can happen quite spontaneously without any yogic training—check themselves into psychiatric wards because they feel something escaping that inside–outside logic, as if part of their experience was floating outside them, sometimes dramatically outside, into the cosmos.[48]

What is germane here is the fear deriving from the constant retweeting of the idea that we are souls or spirits or minds inhabiting a body, like a liquid or a gas in a bottle. It is not merely the mind–body dualism that constitutes the problem here. It resides in the way that dualism is set up, so that one is inside and the other is outside. It all depends on the force and rigidity of the notion of *in*. Yogic practitioners who conjure up kundalini, the serpent energy that rises up the central channel—just in front of your spinal column, according to the manuals—do *tune in* (that word "in" again), attuning their awareness either to unconditional awareness—which cannot be located somewhere at all without losing it—or to a certain specific point in a specific chakra located just below the navel.

What disturbs the people who check themselves into psychiatric wards is how this energy appears to be *moving*, all by itself. The reason the inside–outside distinction becomes ego-threateningly blurry is precisely because of movement—something is moving up, without one's control, like vomiting or excreting, but subtler, until one begins to learn how to tune the radio dial of one's awareness to this faint channel, which people say is thread-like. The more one tunes in, the more intense it seems, becoming physically hot, so much so that some nuns in Nepal and Tibet perform a ritual in which they melt a two-meter radius of snow around their body with this energy. The energy moves up through one's chakras, which are something like psychic sex organs, and they have their own kinds of orgasm—namely they all open as the energy starts to lick around inside them. Bliss is indeed, as Barthes liked to point out, disturbing—and as he failed to point out, it is available within pleasure, which is why esoteric spiritual pathways tend to emphasize pleasure in a way that should remind people of what is disturbing to almost every critical sensibility (Marxisms, some anarchisms, many environmenalisms and so on) about consumerism, which has as its top level the bohemian or Romantic reflexive pursuit of pleasures in a spiritual mode—the politics and poetics of "experience."[49] Eventually the energy opens the chakra at the top of the head and out one goes . . . now, the way to represent this becomes fully paranormal, which is still nowhere near polite or safe to discuss in the spaces of scholarship.[50]

Western scholarship can now say "mindfulness" (a term originating from the discourse of Buddhist meditation) because neoliberalism loves mindfulness. This is for a reason, however, far from that which Žižek assumes, namely that it turns the practitioner into a blissed-out, passive person (like other theorists of the Event, Žižek is averse to passivity). Mindfulness turns the practitioner into a maniacally *active* worker who now has a whole new job to do both at work and at home, namely to remain calm. Scholarship continues to be incapable of saying "awareness," by which meditation manuals mean something effortless, something the practitioner is not "doing" at all, something that occurs more as a self-sustaining flash. This is a shame, because mindfulness is in Buddhist meditation manuals a tool that can allow awareness to happen—at which point the meditator is supposed to drop the mindfulness.

By analogy, one doesn't drive only to demonstrate how adept one is at using the gear lever—unless one is a certain kind of performer of gender. One drives to get somewhere and look out of the window. Suddenly one runs over a dead cat. Mindfulness is like plowing. Awareness is like hunter-gathering. But post-Neolithic humans keep telling themselves that they aren't Paleolithic beings any more, and they keep imagining evoking the Paleolithic as an absurd primitivism or an impossible, sin-exploding return to the gardens of Eden. Instead, we keep cheerleading for the Neolithic, which Jared Diamond calls the worst mistake in the history of the human species.[51]

One doesn't *act* awareness, it happens to one. It seems to have its own kind of existence, from its own side. It is not something you manufacture. Popular contemporary corporate opinion notwithstanding, mindfulness is not definitely good. Often mindfulness can be quite bad. There are people who are very mindful, totally calm, lacking any anxiety, who can even slice things open mindfully. They are called psychopaths. Doing things mindfully is not in and of itself necessarily great, which is why it seems to fit perfectly the murder-suicide culture of neoliberalism.[52] Awareness might occur to a psychopath as the sudden pang of a conscience that she or he never even knew she or he had, experienced like the voice of a god. In short, awareness would appear horribly distorted, like the ghost of Banquo appearing to Macbeth, without bliss. If we reverse engineer from the critique of the hyperactivity of mindfulness, we notice that awareness *rocks* in the sense we are exploring. Awareness oscillates or undulates or vibrates all by itself, neither doing or feeling exclusively, neither active nor passive.

Ecological awareness is knowing that there are a bewildering variety of scales, temporal and spatial, and that the human ones are only a very narrow region of a much larger and necessarily inconsistent and varied scalar possibility space, and that the human scale is not the top scale. Online scale tools and movies that zoom the user smoothly in and out from the Planck length to the scope of the Universe, like being in a private jet of scale, are anthropocentrically scaled, because they interpellate an anthropocentric subject position: the user devours all those scales indiscriminately, like Pac-Man. But reality is scale variant. A rock is a gigantic empty cathedral at a microscopic level; at a nanoscopic level, it is a vast empty region of a solar system. There is no smooth transition zone between these scales, just as in quantum theory there's no energy state "between" specific states—there are blue fields of energy and red fields of energy, figuratively speaking. Phase transitions such as boiling look smooth because of the anthropocentric scale on which one witnesses them. From an electron's point of view, nothing is emergent at all about boiling—there occur sudden jumps in electron orbits, passing over what is in physics called "the forbidden gap." The default theory of action wants a smooth in-between zone because it wants to ascertain how to get from A to B—one wants to be in control of awareness. One wants to be *doing* something, as opposed to *letting something happen*. Online scale tools actually *inhibit* ecological awareness.

On an inhumanly large timescale, rocks behave like liquids, coming and going, moving, shifting, melting. Rocks fail to sit there doing nothing. Humans aren't caught in anthropocentrism without an exit, because they can discern rocks to be liquid, attuning to the timescale on which that liquidity operates, letting it affect them, becoming excited or horrified.

Furthermore, on an inhumanly *small* spatio-temporal scale, tiny slivers of rock vibrate all by themselves. As we observed earlier, they do something much worse for the active–passive binary. They vibrate and not-vibrate at the same time. Operating "between" active and passive, in this quantum theoretical sense, does not mean a smooth nicely put-together compromise in between; it means both/and, and this violates the never-proven (like the existence of a god) but taken-for-gospel logical "Law" of Noncontradiction. The ground state of an entity is this shimmering without mechanical input. Nothing is pushing the little mirror; it just quivers all by itself. It is not passive because it's not being pushed. It fails to be active because it's not doing anything to anything else, in the strictest sense meant in the discourse of physical science: being in a vacuum close to absolute zero. It is satisfying that there is a determinate region just above absolute zero where this starts to happen. The boundary between this phenomenon happening and not happening is neither thin nor rigid, a symptom of determinacy and finitude.

Thinking about action this way is superior to actor-networks or the higher volume version, mechanical pushing-around, which is the scientistic version of Neoplatonic Christianity, the thing that even Descartes (who says he isn't) is retweeting, and the thing that Kant (who says he isn't making the same mistake as Descartes) is also retweeting.[53] This bug has affected many thought domains. Industrial capitalism is theorized by Marx as an emergent property of industrial machines—when you have enough of them, pop![54] But this means that capitalism is like God, always greater than the sum of its parts.

When we bracket off the content, awareness itself appears to be doing something similar to tiny crystals close to absolute zero. Awareness is still and moving at the same time, a ground state of feeling or doing or mentating or being embodied. Awareness rocks. Perhaps meditative awareness is the human version of being a tiny crystal or a massive glacial rock face.

Philosophy requires a new theory of action, a queer one that is neither active nor passive nor a compromised amalgam of both, to help us slip out from underneath physically massive beings such as global warming and neoliberalism, to find some wiggle room down there so we can wriggle or rock our way out of the hyperobjects. This would be a much more interesting and much more powerful revolutionary action theory than, for instance, theories of the Event, which have to do with acting—and damn the torpedoes!— even if history insists it's not going to work right now, enjoining the revolutionary to cut into the continuum because they are the Decider and it's tough at the top, but someone's got to do it . . . Revolutionary action has been malfunctioning, not because it keeps getting appropriated by the system, a thought within cynical reason underwritten by theistic, explosive holism in which the whole is greater than the sum of its parts. What is the case is that the action theories revolution performance embodies tend to be accidentally theistic, and thus they get caught in patriarchal, hierarchical, heteronormative possibility space. If the aesthetic dimension is the causal dimension, attuning-to is not only the possibility condition for acting in the more conventional sense, but also the quantum of action as such.

Love is not straight, because reality is not straight. Everywhere, there are curves and bends, things veer. Per-*ver*-sion. En-*vir*-onment. These terms come from the verb "to veer."[55] To veer, to swerve toward: am I choosing to do so or am I being pulled? Free will is overrated. I do not make decisions outside the Universe and then plunge in, like an Olympic diver. I am already in. I am like a mermaid, constantly pulled and pulling, pushed and pushing, flicked and flicking, turned and opened, moving with the current, pushing away with the force I can muster. An environment is not a neutral, empty box, but an ocean filled with currents and surges.

It's not just that you can have solidarity with nonhumans. It's that solidarity implies nonhumans. Solidarity *requires* nonhumans.

Solidarity just is solidarity with nonhumans.

Notes

INTRODUCTION

1. Curiously, it's a very fine literary-critical essay that illuminates this best: J. Hillis Miller, "The Critic as Host," *Critical Inquiry* 3:3 (Spring 1977), 439–47.
2. J. Bruce German, Samara L. Freeman, Carlito B. Lebrilla and David A. Mills, "Human Milk Oligosaccharides: Evolution, Structures and Bioselectivity as Substrates for Intestinal Bacteria," *PMC*, April 29, 2010, ncbi.nlm.nih.gov, accessed November 8, 2016.
3. Mark T. Boyd, Christopher M. R. Bax, Bridget E. Bax, David L. Bloxam and Robin A. Weiss, "The Human Endogenous Retrovirus ERV-3 is Upregulated in Differentiating Placental Trophoblast Cells," *Virology* 196 (1993), 905–09.
4. Yuval Noah Harari, *Sapiens: A Brief History of Humankind* (New York: Harper, 2015).
5. Felipe Fernández-Armesto, *So You Think You're Human? A Brief History of Humankind* (Oxford and New York: Oxford University Press, 2004), 54.
6. The term was coined by Ernst Haeckel in 1866.
7. Eric Posner and David Weisbach, "Public Policy over Massive Time Scales" (lecture), The History and Politics of the Anthropocene, University of Chicago, May 17–18, 2013.
8. Karl Marx, *Capital*, vol. 1., trans. Ben Fowkes (Harmondsworth: Penguin, 1990), 1.311.

9. Jason W. Moore, *Capitalism in the Web of Life* (London and New York: Verso, 2015).

10. Immanuel Kant, *Critique of Pure Reason*, trans. Paul Guyer and Allen W. Wood (Cambridge and New York: Cambridge University Press, 1998), 169.

11. Theodor Adorno, "Progress," *The Philosophical Forum* 15:1–2 (Fall–Winter 1983–1984), 55–70.

12. *Oxford English Dictionary*, "solidarity," n., oed.com, accessed November 15, 2016.

13. Hunter-gathering worlds involve intricate links between humans and nonhumans to the extent that those categories can be blurred. Terry O'Connor, *Animals as Neighbors: The Past and Present of Commensal Animals* (East Lansing: Michigan State University Press, 2013), 12.

14. Bessel van der Kolk, *The Body Keeps The Score: Brain, Mind, and Body in the Healing of Trauma* (London: Penguin, 2015).

15. Ana Cristina Ramírez Barreto, "Ontology and Anthropology of Interanimality," *Revista de Antropología Iberoamericana* 5:1 (January–April 2010), 32–57.

16. Jean-François Lyotard, *Discourse, Figure*, trans. Antony Hudek and Mary Lydon (Minneapolis: University of Minnesota Press, 2010).

17. Jaleesa Baulkman, "Childhood Exposure to Pet Neglect, Cruelty May Have Similar Lifelong Effect as Domestic Violence," *Medical Daily*, December 9, 2015, medicaldaily.com, accessed January 15, 2016.

18. I use the terms developed by D.W. Winnicott, *Playing and Reality* (New York: Basic Books, 1971). ·

19. Gerald M. Fromm, ed., *Lost in Transmission: Studies of Trauma Across Generations* (London: Karnac Books, 2012).

20. Theodor Adorno, "Progress."

21. Fromm, *Lost in Transmission*, 46–48.

22. Karl Marx, "The Eighteenth Brumaire of Louis Bonaparte," in *Later Political Writings*, trans. Terrell Carver (Cambridge: Cambridge University Press, 1996), 32.

23. Fromm, *Lost in Transmission*, 46–48.

24. Colin N. Waters, Jan Zalasiewicz, et al., "The Anthropocene Is Functionally and Stratigraphically Distinct from the Holocene," *Science* 351:6269 (January 8, 2016).

25. Michael Hardt and Antonio Negri, *Empire* (Cambridge: Harvard University Press, 2000).

26. Alphonso Lingis, *The Community of Those Who Have Nothing in Common* (Bloomington: Indiana University Press, 1994). Jean-Luc Nancy, *The Inoperative Community*, trans. Peter Connor, Lisa Garbus, Michael Holland, and Simona Sawhney (Minneapolis: University of Minnesota Press, 1991).

27. Claude Lévi-Strauss, *Structural Anthropology*, trans. Claire Jacobson and Brooke Grundfest Schoepf (New York: Basic Books, 1963), 134–35. This is well discussed in Slavoj Žižek, *The Parallax View* (Boston: MIT Press, 2006), 25.

28. See Giorgio Agamben, *Homo Sacer: Sovereign Power and Bare Life*, trans. Daniel Heller-Roazen (Stanford: Stanford University Press, 1998).

29. Roland Barthes, "From Work to Text," in *The Rustle of Language*, trans. Richard Howard (New York: Hill and Wange, 1986), 61.

30. Jacques Derrida, *Of Grammatology*, trans. Gayatri Spivak (Baltimore and London: Johns Hopkins University Press, 1987).

31. Erik Loomis, *Out of Sight: The Long and Disturbing Story of Corporations Outsourcing Catastrophe* (New York: The New Press, 2015).

32. Karl Marx, *Economic and Philosophical Manuscripts* in *Early Writings*, trans. Gregor Benton (New York: Penguin, 1992), 349.

33. Bracha Ettinger, "Weaving a Woman Artist with-in the Matrixial Encounter-Event," *Theory, Culture and Society* 21:1 (2004), 69–94.

34. See for example Jonathan Hughes, *Ecology and Historical Materialism* (Cambridge: Cambridge University Press, 2000). Hughes asserts that Marx would have felt contempt for de-anthropocentrism (17).

35. John Bellamy Foster, *Marx's Ecology: Materialism and Nature* (New York: Monthly Review Press, 2000).

36. Norimitsu Onishi, "A Hunting Ban Saps a Village's Livelihood," *New York Times*, September 12, 2015, nytimes.com, accessed October 6, 2016.

37. William Blake, "The Human Abstract," in *The Complete Poetry and Prose of William Blake*, ed. David V. Erdman (New York: Doubleday, 1988), lines 1–2.

38. Ludwig Wittgenstein, *Philosophical Investigations*, trans. G. E. M. Anscombe (Oxford: Blackwell, 1986), 223.

39. I'm very grateful to Kevin MacDonnell for talking this through with me.
40. Adam Smith, *The Theory of Moral Sentiments* (London: A. Millar, 1759).
41. Nicholas Royle, *Telepathy and Literature: Essays on Reading the Mind* (Oxford: Blackwell, 1991).
42. Marx, *Capital*, 1.497.
43. Ibid., 1.375–76.
44. Ibid., 1.556.
45. United Nations, *Agenda 21: The United Nations Programme of Action from Rio* (United Nations, 1992).
46. Timothy Morton, *Hyperobjects: Philosophy and Ecology after the End of the World* (Minneapolis: University of Minnesota Press, 2013).
47. Karl Marx, "Economic and Philosophical Manuscripts," in *Early Writings*, trans. Rodney Livingstone and Gregor Benton, introduction by Lucio Colletti (London: Penguin, 1992), 279–400 (327–28).
48. Ibid., 328–29.

CHAPTER I

1. Martin Hägglund, *Radical Atheism: Derrida and the Time of Life* (Stanford: Stanford University Press, 2008).
2. See Timothy Morton, *Dark Ecology: For a Logic of Future Coexistence* (New York: Columbia University Press, 2016).
3. Bracha Ettinger, "The Laius Complex: Abraham, Laius, Moses; Father, Trauma and Carrying," *Los Angeles Review of Books*, November 8, 2015, lareviewofbooks.org, accessed October 31, 2016.
4. W. F. Ruddiman, et al., "Late Holocene Climate: Natural or Anthropogenic?" *Reviews of Geophysics* 54:1 (March 2016), 93–118.
5. Derek Parfit, *Reasons and Persons* (Oxford and New York: Oxford University Press, 1984).
6. Sigmund Freud, "Beyond the Pleasure Principle," in *Beyond the Pleasure Principle and Other Writings*, trans. John Reddick, introduction by Mark Edmundson (London: Penguin, 2003), 43–102. Mary Daly, *Gyn/Ecology: The Metaethics of Radical Feminism* (Boston: Beacon, 1990).
7. Richard Heinberg, *The End of Growth: Adapting to Our New Economic Reality* (Gabriola Island, British Columbia: New Society Publishers, 2011).

8. Aaron D. O'Connell, M. Hofheinz, M. Ansmann, et al., "Quantum Ground State and Single Phonon Control of a Mechanical Ground Resonator," *Nature* 464 (March 17, 2010), 697–703.
9. Ibn Sina (Avicenna), *Metaphysics*, I.8, 53.13–15. I quote the commonly cited version, which appears to be a translation of *La Métaphysique du Shifa*, Livres I à V, ed. Georges Anawati (Paris: Vrin, 1978), cited for instance in Laurence R. Horn, "Contradiction," in the *Stanford Encyclopedia of Philosophy* (Spring 2014), ed. Edward N. Zalta, plato.stanford.edu, accessed July 15, 2015. The more readily available and recent English translation is by Michael E. Marmura (Provo, UT: Brigham Young University Press, 2005), 43. James Boswell, *Boswell's Life of Johnson* (Oxford: Oxford University Press, 1965).
10. Charles Darwin, *The Origin of Species*, ed. Gillian Beer (Oxford and New York: Oxford University Press, 1996 [1859]).
11. Immanuel Kant, *Critique of Pure Reason*, trans. Norman Kemp Smith (Boston and New York: Bedford/St. Martin's, 1965), 51.

CHAPTER 2

1. William Arntz, Betsy Chasse, and Mark Vicente, dirs., *What the Bleep Do We Know!?* (Samuel Goldwyn Films, 2004).
2. Karen Barad, *Meeting the Universe Halfway: Quantum Physics and the Entanglement of Matter and Meaning* (Durham, NC: Duke University Press, 2007).
3. Lorna Marshall, *Nyae Nyae !Kung Beliefs and Rites* (Cambridge, MA: Peabody Museum Press, 1999).
4. At the time of writing all "loopholes" in the quantum theory of nonlocality have been closed: B. Henson et al., "Experimental Loophole-Free Violation of a Bell Inequality Using Entangled Electron Spins Separated by 1.3km," arXiv:1508.05949, arxiv.org, accessed November 15, 2016.
5. *Oxford English Dictionary*, "spectre," n., oed.com, accessed August 7, 2014.
6. Karl Marx, *Capital*, 3 vols., trans. Ben Fowkes (Harmondsworth: Penguin, 1990), 1.163.
7. Jacques Derrida, *Specters of Marx: The State of the Debt, the Work of Mourning, and the New International*, trans. Peggy Kamuf (London: Routledge, 1994), chapter 7.
8. Marx, *Capital*, 1.1044.

9. Karl Marx, "Notes on Adolph Wagner's 'Lehrbuch der politischen Okonomie' (Second Edition), Volume 1, 1879," marxists.org, accessed October 27, 2016.

10. Marx, *Capital*, 1.163.

11. Ibid., 1.164–165.

12. Aimé Césaire, "Discourse on Colonialism," in *Postcolonial Criticism*, ed. Bart Moore-Gilbert, Gareth Stanton and Willy Maley (New York: Routledge, 1997), 82.

13. A similar point is made concerning the work of Lynn Margulis in Bruce Clarke, "Introduction: Earth, Life, and System," in *Earth, Life, and System: Evolution and Ecology on a Gaian Planet*, Bruce Clarke, ed. (New York: Fordham University Press, 2015), 24–25.

14. Marx, *Capital*, 1.638.

15. Richard Dawkins, *The Extended Phenotype: The Long Reach of the Gene* (Oxford: Oxford University Press, 1999).

16. Marx, *Capital*, 1.620.

17. I concur with Aimé Césaire on decolonization: "Discourse on Colonialism," in *Postcolonial Criticism*, 82.

18. Theodor W. Adorno, *Negative Dialectics*, trans. E. B. Ashton (New York: Continuum, 1973), 5 ("Dialectics is the consistent sense of nonidentity"), 147–48, 149–50.

19. My argument here resembles Jacques Derrida's: "Economimesis," *Diacritics* 11.2 (Summer 1981), 2–25.

20. Karl Marx, *Economic and Philosophical Manuscripts* in *Early Writings*, trans. Rodney Livingstone and Gregor Benton, introduction by Lucio Colletti (London: Penguin, 1992), 279–400 (328).

21. Dawkins, *The Extended Phenotype*.

22. Charles Baudelaire, *Les Fleurs du Mal*, trans. Richard Howard (Brighton: Harvester, 1982).

23. William Shakespeare, *King Lear*, in *The Arden Shakespeare Complete Works*, ed. Richard Proudfoot, Ann Thompson and David Scott Kastan (London: Bloomsbury, 2001), 4.1.38–39.

24. Marx, *Capital*, vol. 1, chapter 15, 492–508 passim, especially 496.

25. Pincelli Hull, Simon Darroch and Douglas Erwin, "Rarity in Mass Extinctions and the Future of Ecosystems," *Nature* 528 (December 17, 2015), 345–51.

26. Paul Crutzen and E. Stoermer, "The Anthropocene," *Global Change Newsletter* 41.1 (2000), 17–18.

27. Jim Shelton, "How to See a Mass Extinction if it's Right In Front of You," *YaleNews*, news.yale.edu, accessed January 23, 2016.

28. Luce Irigaray, *This Sex Which Is Not One*, trans. Catherine Porter and Carolyn Burke (Ithaca, NY: Cornell University Press, 1985).

29. Sigmund Freud, *The Uncanny*, trans. David McClintock and Hugh Haughton (London: Penguin, 2003).

30. Karl Marx, "The Eighteenth Brumaire of Louis Bonaparte," in *Later Political Writings*, trans. Terrell Carver (Cambridge: Cambridge University Press, 1996), 32.

31. Ibid., 34.

32. Martin Heidegger, *Being and Time*, trans. Joan Stambaugh (Albany, NY: State University of New York Press, 1996), 199–200.

33. Giorgio Agamben, *The Open: Man and Animal*, trans. Kevin Attell (Stanford, CA: Stanford University Press, 2004).

34. Carl Safina, *Beyond Words: What Animals Think and Feel* (New York: Henry Holt, 2015), 81.

35. Ibid., 29.

36. The comedian Stephen Colbert's term really is very useful.

37. John Keats, "In Drear-Nighted December," in *The Complete Poems*, ed. John Barnard, (London: Penguin, 1987), line 21.

38. Hettie MacDonald, dir., "Blink," *Doctor Who*, BBC, June 9, 2007.

39. Aristotle, *Metaphysics*, trans. and introduction by Hugh Lawson-Tancred (London: Penguin, 2004), 213, 217.

40. "In utter contrast to these people obsessed with total explanation, the Achuar make no effort at all to bestow upon the world a coherence that it manifestly lacks." Philippe Descola, *The Spears of Twilight: Life and Death in the Amazon Jungle* (New York: The New Press, 1998), 224.

41. The Beatles, "A Day in the Life," *Sgt. Pepper's Lonely Hearts Club Band* (Parlophone, 1967).

42. Markus Gabriel, *Why the World Does Not Exist* (Malden, MA: Polity Press, 2015)

43. Safina, *Beyond Words*, 284–85.

44. Michael Mountain, "Lawsuit Filed Today on Behalf of Chimpanzee Seeking Legal Personhood," Nonhuman Rights Project, December 2, 2013, nonhumanrightsproject.org, accessed October 31, 2016.

CHAPTER 3

1. I am grateful to Luke Jones for discussing this with me.
2. Emily Stewart, "German Village Feldheim the Country's First Community to Become Energy Self-Sufficient," *Australian Broadcasting Corporation*, November 10, 2014, abc.net.au, accessed October 31, 2016. Hermann Scheer, *The Solar Economy: Renewable Energy and a Sustainable Future* (New York: Routledge, 2004).
3. Mikhail Bakunin, *God and the State* (English translation, 1883), chapter 2, marxists.org, accessed November 5, 2016.
4. Jason Van Vleet, dir., *Terror from Within: The Untold Story Behind the Oklahoma City Bombing*, (Los Angeles: MGA Films, 2003).
5. Georg Wilhelm Friedrich Hegel, *Hegel's Aesthetics: Lectures on Fine Art*, 2 vols., trans. T. M. Knox, (Oxford: Oxford University Press, 2010), 1.516–29; *Introductory Lectures on Aesthetics*, trans. Bernard Bosanquet, introduction and commentary by Michael Inwood (London: Penguin, 1993), 85–86.
6. Slavoj Žižek on *Alien: Resurrection* in Sophie Fiennes, dir., *The Pervert's Guide to Cinema* (ICA Projects, 2006).
7. Karl Marx, *Grundrisse: Foundations of the Critique of Political Economy*, trans. and introduction Martin Nicolaus (London: Penguin, 1993), 111.
8. Percy Bysshe Shelley, "The Mask of Anarchy," in *Poetical Works*, ed. Thomas Hutchinson (New York: Oxford University Press, 1970).

CHAPTER 4

1. Christophe Bonneuil and Jean-Baptiste Fressoz, *The Shock of the Anthropocene: The Earth, History and Us*, trans. David Fernbach (London: Verso, 2016).
2. Immanuel Kant, *Anthropology from a Pragmatic Point of View*, ed. Robert B. Louden, introduction by Manfred Kuehn (Cambridge: Cambridge University Press, 2006), 416–17.
3. Slavoj Žižek, "The Cologne Attacks were an Obscene Version of Carnival," *New Statesman*, January 13, 2016, newstatesman.com, accessed January 15, 2016.
4. Norman Geras, *Marx and Human Nature: Refutation of a Legend* (London: Verso, 2016).

5. Karl Marx, "Notes on Adolph Wagner's *Lehrbuch der Politischen Ökonomie* (Second Edition), Volume 1, 1879," marxists.org, accessed Oct 27, 2016.
6. Derek Parfit, *Reasons and Persons* (Oxford: Oxford University Press, 1984), 355–57.
7. Peter Wade, *Race: An Introduction* (Cambridge: Cambridge University Press, 2015), chapter 2.
8. Freud, *The Uncanny*.

CHAPTER 5

1. Max Stirner, *The Ego and His Own*, trans. Stephen T. Byington, introduction by J. L. Walker (New York: Benjamin R. Tucker, 1907), 34; available at theanarchistlibrary.org, accessed November 5, 2016.
2. A very vivid visualization occurs in Bracha Ettinger, "Copoesis," *Ephemera* 5:X (2005), 703–13.
3. John Keats, Letter to Richard Woodhouse, October 27, 1818, in *John Keats: Selected Letters*, ed. Robert Gittings and Jon Mee (Oxford: Oxford University Press, 2002), 147–48 (148).
4. Christopher Nolan, dir., *Interstellar* (Paramount, 2014).
5. Ken Burns, dir., *The Dust Bowl* (PBS, 2012).
6. Two authors call it "nafthism" after a Greek term for oil: Antti Salminen and Tere Vadén, *Energy and Experience: An Essay in Nafthology* (Chicago: MCM´, 2015), 25–27.
7. Jeffrey Kripal, *Authors of the Impossible: The Paranormal and the Sacred* (Chicago: University of Chicago Press, 2010).
8. Jacques Lacan, "The Agency of the Letter in the Unconscious," *Ecrits: A Selection*, trans. Alan Sheridan (London: Tavistock, 1977), 146–78 (166).
9. George Musser, "Let's Rethink Space: Does Space Exist without Objects, or Is It Made by Them?" *Nautilus 32* (January 14, 2016), nautil.us, accessed October 24, 2016.
10. John Cleese and Graham Chapman, "Argument Clinic," *Monty Python's Flying Circus* (BBC, 1972).
11. Max Baginski, "Without Government," *Mother Earth* 1:1 (March 1906), gutenberg.org, accessed November 5, 2016.
12. Stirner, *The Ego and His Own*, 12.
13. Ibid., 13.

14. Ibid., 30–31.

15. Ibid., 34; see also 35.

16. "Progress," *The Philosophical Forum* 15.1–2 (Fall–Winter 1983–1984), 55–70.

17. Friedrich Engels, "Natural Science in the Spirit World," *Dialectics of Nature*, ed. Yuri Vasin in Karl Marx and Friedrich Engels, *Collected Works*, vol. 25, trans., Emile Burns and Clemens Dutt, Natalia Karmanova, Margarita Lopukhina, Mzia Pitskhelauri, Andrei Skvarsky and Georgi Bagaturia, eds. (Moscow: Progress Publishers, 1987), 345–55.

18. Theodor Adorno, "Theses Against Occultism," *Minima Moralia: Reflections from Damaged Life*, trans. E. P. N. Jephcott (London: Verso, 2005), 238.

19. María del Pilar Blanco and Esther Peeren, "Introduction: Conceptualizing Spectralities," in María del Pilar Blanco and Esther Peeren, eds., *The Spectralities Reader: Ghosts and Haunting in Contemporary Cultural Theory* (London: Bloomsbury, 2013), 5.

20. Karl Marx, *Capital*, vol. 1, trans. Ben Fowkes (Harmondsworth: Penguin, 1990).

21. Theodor Adorno, "Sur l'Eau," *Minima Moralia: Reflections from Damaged Life*, trans. E. F. N. Jephcott (London: Verso, 1978), 155–57 (157).

22. Herman Melville, "Bartleby, the Scrivener," in *Billy Budd, Sailor and Selected Tales*, ed. Robert Milder (Oxford: Oxford University Press, 1998), 41.

23. Adorno, "Sur l'Eau," 155–57 (157).

24. Safina, *Beyond Words*.

25. Bruce Clarke, "Introduction: Earth, Life, and System," in Bruce Clarke, ed., *Earth, Life, and System: Evolution and Ecology on a Gaian Planet* (New York: Fordham University Press, 2015), 19.

26. Lauren Davis, "Why Everything You Know about Wolf Packs Is Wrong," *iO9*, May 12, 2015, io9.gizmodo.com, accessed June 29, 2016.

27. Peter Kropotkin, *Mutual Aid: A Factor of Evolution* (The Anarchist Library, 1902), 6.

28. With "companion species" I evoke Donna Haraway, *When Species Meet* (Minneapolis: University of Minnesota Press, 2007).

29. Kropotkin, *Mutual Aid*, 8, 18, 27.

30. Ibid., 68, 148, 159.

31. Jan Sapp, *Evolution by Association: A History of Symbiosis* (Oxford: Oxford University Press, 1994).

32. Gillian Beer, "Introduction," in Charles Darwin, *The Origin of Species* (Oxford: Oxford University Press, 1998), vii–xxviii (xxvii–xviii).

33. Engels, *Dialectics of Nature*, 452–64 (460).

34. Kropotkin, *Mutual Aid*, 32.

35. Ahmed Farag Ali and Saurya Das, "Cosmology from Quantum Potential," Physics Letters B741 (2015).

36. *Oxford English Dictionary*, "rock," v.1, oed.com, accessed October 23, 2016.

37. Viktor Schklovsky, *Theory of Prose*, trans. Benjamin Sher, introduction by Gerald L. Burns (Normal, IL: Dalkey Archive Press, 1991), 15.

38. I draw here on Martin Heidegger's concept of the nonhuman realm in the worldview of technology as "*Bestand*," standing-reserve. Martin Heidegger, "The Question Concerning Technology," in *Basic Writings: From 'Being and Time' (1927) to 'The Task of Thinking' (1964)*, ed. David Farrell Krell (New York: HarperCollins Publishers, 1993), 307–41.

39. In David Toop, *Haunted Weather: Music, Silence and Memory* (London: Serpent's Tail, 2004), 239–40.

40. Engels, *Dialectics of Nature*, 461.

41. Brian Eno, sleeve note, *Ambient 1: Music for Airports* (EG Records, 1978).

42. Joey Negro, "Do What You Feel," 12" (Ten Records, 1991).

43. Quartz, "Meltdown," 12" (ITM Music, 1989).

44. Reese, "Rock to the Beat (Mayday Mix)," *Rock to the Beat* (KMS Records, 1989).

45. Jack Halberstam, "An Introduction to Gothic Monstrosity," in Robert Louis Stevenson, *The Strange Case of Dr. Jekyll and Mr. Hyde: An Authoritative Text, Backgrounds and Contexts, Performance Adaptations, Criticism*, ed. Katherine Linehan (New York: Norton, 2003), 128–31.

46. Nicolas Abraham and Mária Török, *The Wolf Man's Magic Word: A Cryptonymy*, trans. Nicholas Rand, foreword by Jacques Derrida (Minneapolis: University of Minnesota Press, 2005).

47. Jacques Derrida, "Violence and Metaphysics," *Writing and Difference*, trans. Alan Bass (London and Henley: Routledge and Kegan Paul, 1978), 79–153 (151–52).

48. Stanislav Grof, *Spiritual Emergency: When Personal Transformation Becomes a Crisis* (New York: Tarcher, 1989).

49. "Understanding Traditional and Modern Patterns of Consumption in Eighteenth-Century England: A Character-Action Approach," in John Brewer and Roy Porter, eds., *Consumption and the World of Goods* (London and New York: Routledge, 1993), 40–57.

50. Jeffrey Kripal, *The Serpent's Gift: Gnostic Reflections on the Study of Religion* (Chicago: University of Chicago Press, 2006).

51. Jared Diamond, "The Worst Mistake in the History of the Human Race," *Discover Magazine* (May 1987), 64–66.

52. Franco "Bifo" Berardi, *Heroes: Mass Murder and Suicide* (London: Verso, 2015).

53. Martin Heidegger, *What Is a Thing?*, trans. W. B. Barton and Vera Deutsch, analysis by Eugene T. Gendlin (Chicago: Henry Regnery, 1967).

54. Marx, *Capital*, vol. 1, chapter 15.

55. Nicholas Royle, *Veering: A Theory of Literature* (Edinburgh: Edinburgh University Press, 2011).

Index